W. H. Carpenter

BEYOND SUCCESS AND FAILURE

4 Clematis Court
Sumter

To George + Gordon

Love
Bill 1989

*Also by Willard and Marguerite Beecher*

PARENTS ON THE RUN: *The Need for Discipline in Parent-Child and Teacher-Child Relationships*

# *Beyond Success and Failure*

WAYS TO SELF-RELIANCE AND MATURITY » *Willard and Marguerite Beecher*

WILLARD & MARGUERITE BEECHER FOUNDATION

DALLAS, TEXAS

*Library of Congress Catalog Card Number: 66-24877*
*Published by The Julian Press, Inc.*
*119 Fifth Avenue, New York, N. Y. 10003*
*Manufactured in the United States of America*
*by H. Wolff, New York*
*Design: Cynthia Muser*

*Second Printing, February 1967*

*Revised Edition, 1986*
*ISBN: 0-87516-569-9*

*Distributed by*
*DeVorss & Company*
*P.O. Box 550*
*Marina del Rey, CA 90294*

CONTENTS

## CHARTS

BEYOND SUCCESS AND FAILURE

# *Introduction*

Self-help books have been notoriously ineffectual in helping people, for the most part. It is important to understand why this is so. Past efforts have been based on the positive approach, which is an additive process. It assumes the reader is empty and the problem exists as a lack of pertinent information that can be supplied to him as in a cookbook with recipes for various situations. Some authors give case histories, which serve as horrible examples of the various aberrations—a kind of rogues' gallery of evils. This method seldom worked, as hardly anyone was able to find a case just like his own, and thus could not profit by what he found. Another approach has been largely inspirational, built on exhortation or encouragement to urge the failing individual to greater efforts to lift his goals higher and keep striving for them. But tugging on his own bootstraps didn't help the poor fellow either. He felt held back by something. Or his boots were stuck in the mud somewhere. The high resolves fired by the inspiration and exhortation faded into his old level of discouragement, and old symptoms came back. The fires of influence and inspiration became merely embers, then transient dreams that later increased the original feeling of discouragement and inadequacy.

The positive approach assumes that the mind is an unwritten page waiting for someone to write on it. Or better still, an Empty Mug waiting for the Big Jug to pour wisdom into it! People in need of help avidly read such books with great hope and conscientiously try to remember all the valuable information laid down in them. But it is not possible to pour anything into a full cup. It simply runs over the top! The person who has carefully remembered all the admonitions feels quite confident, until he meets an old situation he is afraid of. In panic he tries to remember which of the many inspiring bits of information he is supposed to use to slay the on-coming dragon. His mind goes blank, and he meets the situation in his old, familiar, habitual, unsatisfactory way. As the tuba player said, "I breathe in so sweet—but it comes out so sour"!

If we wish to achieve any fundamental change in our character, it is quite futile to depend on information, sermons, and lectures as a solution of the problem. We immediately run into the old stone wall of habit. And habit never rests! The mind is filled with misconceptions, which add up to *dependency on outside authority figures*. The misconceptions must be destroyed. It is simply not possible to alter oneself—*to go beyond old conditioning—without first destroying the compulsive hold that habit has on us*. There must be a period of unlearning, so that the person can de-condition himself to his old, habitual responses.

Experience has taught us not to expect to keep our New Year's resolutions! Within a few days or weeks we fall back into our old levels. We greatly underestimate how much of our life is built around our "bad" habits and the joy they give us. We do not want to give them up in the first place; we want *only to rid ourselves of the pain they cost us*. The alcoholic who gives up drinking is suddenly and shockingly faced with an empty, lonely life. He does not know what to do with himself when he is not drinking, as most of his leisure time was spent drinking and almost all of his friends were drinkers like himself. He is suddenly filled with the horrors of sobriety and *without anything to put into the vacuum left* when he took the bottle out of his life.

The person who wants to change his habits must first

reckon with his present host and pay his bill before he can be free of the debt he has to old conditioning. His job is to empty out the old garbage—not try to fill in on top of it! The job is much like that of building a modern structure on the site of an old shack. The old encumbrance has to be removed to make way for the new. When the old mistaken certainties and old dependencies from childhood have been cleared out, then the way opens for new behavior by itself, without any pressure on our part.

In the light of the above, the term "self-help" is, in a sense, a misnomer. It implies the exclusive application of some will or effort. As we see, however, we need only to discover and destroy mistakes and illusions that fog the mind. When we have seen accurately the What Is in a situation, everything turns right-side up by itself, as it ought to be. Nothing new has to be learned or practiced.

A world in which a man cannot help himself is quite unthinkable! To whom shall a man turn if he cannot trust himself? Is he doomed to face life waiting for some outside salvation that may never come? Are most of us doomed to futility because not enough professionals can ever be trained to save us from ourselves? Is there a way by which we can use our own existing powers to help ourselves? Did nature provide a factor within each of us for his own salvation? It must be so, at least at the psychological level. Two great teachers thought so. When Buddha came upon his own enlightenment, he said, "Be a lamp unto your own feet; do not seek outside yourself." Jesus was of the same opinion when he said, "The Kingdom of Heaven is not 'lo here' nor 'lo there'; it is within." The great sages of all time seem to agree that a man cannot turn to someone else to save himself—that the answer lies within his reach and in his own inner endowments. Each has been given the medicine with which to cure himself. It would be an unjust world indeed if this were not the situation.

»

A person must never feel he is in a situation where life overwhelms him or that he is not able to help himself. Feelings of helplessness and loneliness, fear and despair sweep over the person who believes he cannot meet the demands of life. His despair frequently leads to desperation. This is especially true if he does not know where to turn in his confusion. What does one do when he hits the panic button? What is a person to do if he cannot trust himself when things are rough?

Technological knowledge and techniques multiply faster all the while, and miracles are performed daily in the physical world of things. But there has been no corresponding progress in our understanding of ways to help ourselves when we are hurt emotionally, at the psychological level. There is a babel of voices of outside authorities in our ears, but it seldom helps when things get too hot for us to handle in our daily lives. We lose confidence in ourselves and begin to run in all directions for an escape from the threat of pressing events. Life is like driving in the face of on-coming traffic. We must be able to do it easily without anxiety or we risk damage. We must develop *full trust of our own inherent capacities* and not flee in panic from the scene.

There is, however, a widespread belief that an individual must seek the help of some professional adviser if he is in chronic emotional difficulty and wants to change. Many people believe that their problems are so deep that no solution is possible to them on their own understanding and initiative. They believe that they are doomed to a lifetime of unhappiness unless they can find the right person to relieve them from the psychological bind in which they find themselves. Fortunately for all of us, nature built into each person his own self-healing powers, both at the physical and psychological level. Health is the natural state of being, and it restores itself *when we refrain from habits that interfere with it.*

When World War II began, the armed forces suddenly discovered they had a large number of men with serious emotional problems who were incapable of useful service. Something had to be done for them even before discharging them from the service. But there were not enough trained personnel to handle even a fraction of them on the customary basis of individual treatment.

Something had to be improvised on a group basis, although no trained personnel existed to do any amount of group therapy. In desperation an experiment was tried. Groups of emotionally disturbed persons were formed and encouraged to discuss their individual difficulties together informally. Astonishing things began to happen in such groups. Without any formal treatment or the application of any method or theory, large numbers of men made big strides in freeing themselves of the bonds that had been holding them.

At the same time around the country, alcoholics heard of a remarkable organization called Alcoholics Anonymous, which was working miracles simply by group participation and discussion. Most of those who joined it found themselves dry of alcohol and repairing the shambles into which their lives had fallen. Here again were individuals who were lifting themselves by their bootstraps. Even those alcoholics who had had professional care without any improvement now found that they were doing on their own what they had believed impossible for them to do.

Since then, this self-help approach to one's own problems has extended to gambling, narcotics, obesity and similar addictions. In each of these areas self-help has accomplished results that seem like a miracle to the person who was suffering. These pioneers demonstrated a very exciting fact—that addictions may be of long standing, but they are not deep in the sense that they *cannot be handled at the level of everyday living by the individual.*

The fact that one can free himself of crippling neurosis, then, has been shown by countless persons who had a variety of symptoms of all degrees of intensity. In fact, this approach works best when the person is suffering so much that he is "happy to do anything—even get well." Professional treatment has a role to play in many situations and need not be ignored. But anyone who is sincerely ready to get out of his own trap can escape by increasing his own self-understanding.

It is not always possible to find a group of like-minded individuals who will form a discussion group with us in our quest for understanding. But fortunately for everyone, there are many mistaken certainties that are to be found as a hard core, or least common denominator, in most—if not all—emotional difficulties. A mistaken certainty is something described as "something you are sure is so—but ain't." We shall describe the most important of these mistakes and how they act as partially submerged obstructions to our plans. These mistaken certainties are at the root of wishful thinking, which leads us to self-deception "to make our dream come true." We view the world through a cloud of wishes and distort reality, so that we are blind to things as they *really happen*. The wish for ideal conditions makes us wish to be blind to reality, which we then avoid in favor of pleasurable illusions and the pursuit of greatness.

Self-deception denies reality. But when the pain grows great enough, reality insists on breaking through. At such a time, when a man is lost, he needs a map—not a formula or method. Systems of "do and don't" will not help him find his way. Such authoritarian systems of positive and negative commands fail immediately when he tries to function with them. Nothing other than a free mind will provide the autonomy and spontaneity that life demands of us. To free the mind of wishful thinking must become the central aim of all our thinking. Only that will lead us past the Scylla and Charybdis of the illusion of success and failure.

Each of us has an intuitive feeling that he has a central core that is not ill and cannot be touched by the evils that may be tearing at his flesh. We somehow are not surprised when we are told for the first time that at the eye of the hurricane is total calm, a place where the sun is shining and the birds are singing. We know that somewhere inside of us we are at peace. Our only problem is to discover what prevents us from getting to this center-of-our-being and holding on to it. The question in our mind is why we cannot live at this core easily, as we know it must be possible for a man to do.

That is the concern of this book. It is not a how-to-do-it book. A man does not have to create this core in himself, because it is there *sui generis,* a gift inherent from birth. Nor does he have to learn how to seek it by some arduous discipline or self-denial. What he needs to know is that mysterious factors alienate us or seem to drag us off this center.

When these "gravitational pulls" are taken off us, we discover we are at the center-of-our-being and had never departed from it, but that we had been blinded by the storm of our distortions and illusions. The important theme of this book is that we do not have to learn *some new discipline* to arrive at our own center—because we never departed from it. We were only the victims of our illusions about the world. These led us to feel we had abdicated our rights or drifted off course. *Reality appears immediately after our illusions are destroyed.*

The negative approach to reality is the *destruction of illusion.* The positive approach is a confusion of multiple do's and don't's that blur the mind with contradictions and inconsistencies. The negative approach, fortunately, is only concerned with regaining our original ability to see and hear the What Is of a situation without it being *distorted, edited* or *judged* by our habit of wishful thinking. The fall of man in the *Old Testament* is described as happening at that moment when he aspires "to become as if a God, knowing both good and evil"—that is, when he wants to be a big shot. When we can distinguish wishful thinking and the illusions it creates from What Is, we are saved.

This is not a book in the ordinary sense. It has no beginning and no end; it doesn't go anywhere. It is more in the nature of a map of What Is on which one can chart shoals and reefs of illusion that abound in the sea of life. Try to look at What Is dispassionately and with total acceptance in your own life.

»

It was Thoreau's opinion that most people live lives of quiet desperation. And from appearances, it seems that this may be all too near the truth. Does life condemn most of us to defeat and frustration in this world? Is this the basic nature of things which only a few fortunate individuals may hope to escape? Are these fortunates elected for what we call "success"? And are the rest of us fated to be nonentities and to dwell in the shadows with tedious, undistinguished, alienated lives? Or is our unhappiness really nothing more than a complaint we make about our own character? Is unhappiness due to our way of looking at ourselves and the world around us? Are we perennial victims of a hostile outside world, or does each of us have an equal chance for happiness, regardless of such accidents of birth as wealth, learning, race, religion or nationality? These are basic questions that must be answered by each of us as to whether we continue to live as victims or whether, by the exercise of our own understanding and initiative, we can perform Operation Bootstrap and live as first-class citizens who put *no head higher* than our own!

If we are not victims struggling in a hostile world, then many of us face the problem of getting "unbugged," so that we no longer see hostility and behave in a hostile manner. We must undertake the process of *un*learning whatever habit it is that leads us to our dismal outlook and customary feelings of depression. We must learn *to see* and *to hear outside* our old, habitual way of looking at the world and at those around us.

One of the most destructive distortions we endlessly encounter is the illusion of success and failure. It gives rise to the driving desire to get ahead and become somebody. Some people are so blinded by this ilusion they cannot imagine anything could exist apart from their endless struggle to get ahead in order to be "one up" on those around them. Those who feel they cannot get ahead regard themselves as failures and feel there is no reason to keep on living if they cannot find success.

Can this be *all* of life? Surely there has to be another, less hostile way of life which is not based wholly on competition. The world of success and failure is based on appearances or the semblance of things—not on reality.

Like Alice in *Through the Looking-Glass,* we must go behind the mirror, beyond the appearance of success and failure before we can find reality.

The individual trapped in the struggle for prestige, recognition and appearances, is a helpless victim of his own wishful thinking. He is trapped in ideas of what should-be or what ought-to-be—ideally. Such wishful thinking is a basic *illness of the mind.* Only when we transcend such a habit of mind can we hope to go beyond this trap and discover *our own essential nature.* The person who escapes this competitive struggle is a person with a free mind. He is often called a sage. Such free individuals are unfortunately rare among us—even though *each of us has this potential as a birthright alive inside him, waiting only to be released.* We need not envy others who clearly have discovered it. It is easy to see this quality of the free mind if we look through the eyes of Walt Whitman in "Leaves of Grass" as he gazes admiringly at animals who share this birthright:

> *I think I could turn and live with animals, they are so*
> *placid and self-contained;*
> *I stand and look at them long and long.*
> *They do not sweat and whine about their condition.*
> *They do not lie awake in the dark and weep for their*
> *sins;*
> *They do not make me sick discussing their duty to God.*

*Not one is dissatisfied, not one is demented with the mania of owning things.*
*Not one kneels to another, nor to his kind that lived thousands of years ago.*
*Not one is respectable or industrious over the whole earth.*

We dedicate this book to the late Dr. Alfred Adler, founder of Individual Psychology, who was our teacher the last years of his life, during which time he gave us our first understanding of human behavior. We learned from him essentially:

1 That the individual's approach to life is a result of early self-training due to his interpretation of his situation. He can change it in later years only if he realizes that his disturbing, conditioned responses are nothing more than inappropriate, inadequate holdovers from childhood. The adult is expected to replace such behavior with more useful responses to be a help and not a burden. He should realize it is useless to try to escape the pain he creates for himself trying to solve adult problems with a child's tricks and evasions, since problems are only situations for which we have not trained ourselves.

2 That the problems of behavior, which make us feel and act like inferior second-class passengers in life,

are no more than the results of our failure to develop the habit of both emotional and physical self-reliance; we retain from childhood the mistaken expectation that others should "hold up our pants" for us emotionally and physically and be interested in as well as responsible for our welfare.

3 That leaning on others emotionally or physically is a child's way of life. We should not permit this habit to follow us into adult life, since dependency is the root of all feelings of inferiority. Dependency generates the feeling of second-class citizenship. Out of this grows the habit of competition, envy, making comparisons and similar mistaken compensatory striving that we create in our effort to assuage the pain of feeling second class in relation to others. Humiliating feelings of inferiority produce the gnawing, distracting, disruptive, destructive craving for personal recognition and prestige, with its inescapable fear of failure.

4 That unhappiness, loneliness, neurotic symptoms, crime and similar distresses *arise directly* from this unresolved habit of leaning and depending on others whom we immediately feel we must try to control, rule, dominate or exploit for our own benefit, since we cannot otherwise support ourselves physically and emotionally.

5 That only those who are self-reliant emotionally and physically can function as *adult* human beings able to cooperate with other adults, because life demands that we be useful and productive or, as Adler said, to "be a help and not a burden."

6 That the inadequate responses of envy, greed, competition and sabotage—with which we try to solve confronting problems of life—are only reactions *which would not arise in the first place* if we were in the habit of standing on our own feet and were not always trying to find someone on whom to lean and exploit, demanding that they prop us up and hold us there.

7 That defects of self-reliance and the *inescapable pain* that accompanies them can be changed only when we *fully realize* that the pain we suffer is but the other-end-of-the-stick of our leaning, dependent, subaltern habits of mind. Our problems do not have mysterious, hidden sources, and we do not have to look far or deep to find the source; we keep stumbling, tripping and falling over it all day long, even though we refuse to identify it as our own childishness.

8 That all human beings are the product of evolution, and that we share the inheritance of all human potentialities and are equally based in evolution. Each can evoke his store of potentialities to shape them into his *own creation* and discover his own reality. Each is his own architect. Whatever one human being has done can be done by others. Creation is a built-in attribute of each of us. It waits, however, for the awakening touch of self-reliance to shape its parts and aspects.

# BEYOND SUCCESS AND FAILURE / I

# *1 / The feeling of deprivation*

How is one to know when he is in a dangerous situation of dependency? What warning signal has nature provided us so that we know when we are leaning, expecting, envying, comparing or begging? How shall we know when we have abdicated our own initiative and have put another head higher than our own? Is there an unmistakable sign that always accompanies dependency, so that we immediately know when we have stepped backward into the child's passive-receptive approach to life instead of maintaining an adult, active and productive role?

Fortunately, such a signal exists. It is quite unmistakable, and its effect is as immediate as when a small cloud passes over the face of the sun on a summer day. A person feels expansive, confident and adequate while he is in his active self-reliant phase. But the moment he compares himself to someone, whose head he puts higher than his own, he feels a chill. He is suddenly aware that he feels deprived, empty, lonely, weak, defenseless, inadequate, put back or frightened. Just as if he had suddenly lost his power to meet life, and the situation in front of him seems dangerous or, at the best, unrewarding. The feeling of contentment has suddenly disappeared.

The feeling of being deprived and put back in life is such a common difficulty that many believe it is a thing-in-itself. They do not realize that it is merely a symptom of the leaning, dependent, subaltern attitude of mind. They are accustomed to this cloud hanging over them, even though things may be going well for them in everyday life. They are aware that they feel unfavored and lack joy in what they are doing. But if they try to think what it is that they are specifically deprived of, they are at a loss to decide on any one thing that they can blame for their unhappiness.

This persistent feeling of being put back and impoverished leads them to seek things to blame for their feeling of depression and discontent. They search their memory for causes of this unhappiness. Some even become accomplished "injustice collectors" in their effort to rationalize and validate to themselves and others why they feel unhappy when there is nothing actively upsetting them at the time.

Such a person tries vainly to tinker with and adjust these imagined causes, or to pay back those who have been "unjust" to him. But regardless of what he does to free himself of his feeling of deprivation, the painful feeling persists and he is unable to either understand or get rid of it. He continues to search for something he can regard as causing the feeling of emptiness and boredom, always hoping that he can fill the aching gap and free himself from pain.

The trap in which his understanding is caught is his lack of understanding that he is *fighting a symptom.* "Feelings are not reasons," said the late Dr. Alfred Adler. The feeling of deprivation does not have a cause in the sense that we are underprivileged in the present situation where we feel the pain. It is the emotional concomitant or result of lacking self-reliance. You can't have a lack of self-reliance without having the feeling of being underprivileged and undervalued. They are the front and back of the same thing.

In substance, the feeling of being deprived is the memory of the old pain of self-pity which we experienced as children when our desires were frustrated. As memory of old pain, we conjure it up out of our mind any time we make a comparison and feel someone is getting along better than we are. We use this pain to stimulate our competitiveness and our infantile acquisitiveness, so that we will take some action and not let others get ahead of us in life. We evoke homicidal, or self-destructive, feelings and use them to right the wrong we fancy has been done to us. but this destructive feeling is nothing more than the old habit of mind we developed in childhood vis-à-vis our siblings. It has no relation to actual deprivation any more than we can have actual pain in a severed limb.

There is a curious resemblance between the feeling of deprivation and a phenomenon known as "phantom limb." An individual who has suffered agony with a limb and then had it amputated may not be free of pain in that limb. In reality, he is suffering only *remembered* pain, but it is as real as if the limb were still attached to his body. Comparison activates the response of infantile acquisitiveness which, in turn, summons this feeling of impoverishment. This induces the tension of greed, and greed is only the other face of, and inseparable from, the feeling of impoverishment.

Dependency always degrades. It degrades by mutual enslavement of both the dependent and the one on whom he leans. *Both are equally guilty* of dependence. The individual who is physically and psychologically self-reliant will not allow anyone to lean on him, as it would result in his enslavement if he permitted it. It becomes evident, then, that the one who leans and the one who allows himself to be leaned on are equally lacking in self-sufficiency. They are in a kind of mutual admiration society, which amounts to a conspiracy to exploit each other. Both are in a condition of second-class citizenship, although one may imagine himself mistakenly as the strong one in the relationship. The fact remains that they degrade, inhibit and enslave each other and that, in such cases, "two is less than one."

Dependency, we must remember at all times, is most of all a habit of mind; it is an habitual approach to confronting problems in which we look outside the self for answers and support instead of finding our own inner direction. Dependency masquerades in an infinite number of ways, so that it can appear to be something else. It can even masquerade as its opposite! In contrariness, it pretends to be self-determination and behaves as if the person had a mind of his own instead of being merely negatively dependent on, and in rebellion against, what is expected of him.

Liberation from the degradation of dependency is not possible unless we can identify the multiple forms of dependence as they arise to make claims on us. We tend to collect dependencies as a boat collects barnacles on its bottom. And their effect on our lives is much the same. Only by developing full awareness of them can we deal with the distortion they bring. But as long as we have not identified the masks they wear, we cannot escape being a victim of them. Our most important task is to maintain constant watch and unmask them as they arise. Habit never rests.

# 2 / *The tragedy of suggestibility*

The ultimate tragedy of dependency is that the dependent individual does not develop his inborn ability to bring his own powers into focus and direct them to solve his own problems. We are all born with the same human potentialities. But the dependent individual has not developed the self-reliance that acts as a catalytic agent to evoke and combine innate powers and release them in activity. When the leaning individual is confronted, he is helpless and must search for someone on whom to lean for help in the solution of his problems. Looking about for assistance opens him to all the evils of suggestibility and uncertainty. He vainly runs from one person to another, like a lost dog at a parade looking for his master to lead him safely home again. The dependent, enslaved mind dares not stand alone.

The free mind, on the other hand, is not distracted by the need to find a master on whom to lean. It moves spontaneously on target to deal with the situation. Its function is automatic because it has not been contaminated by the habit of wishful thinking; it is content to look directly at the What Is of the here-and-now and is able to deal with things as they are—not as they ought to be in some idealized but nonexistent situation. The free mind is not trapped by a desire to edit, escape, distort, change or evade what it faces and thus postpone movement or the solution of the problem. It has no need to take endless thought and fall into a quandary in which the mind consults the mind about the mind. It does not need to look outside itself for either help or stimulation. As we have seen earlier, the free mind manipulates impersonal circumstance—not people.

The leaning, dependent mind, however, is at the mercy of outside stimulation and outside support. Every voice it hears is magnified into the voice of authority which must be obeyed. Each suggestion becomes a command, and every person becomes ten feet tall. This abject suggestibility condemns the individual to the role of a subordinate, and he is subject to all the commands tossed at him. The opinions of other people are as a missile—and he feels himself the only target.

The dependent mind is in a constant state of near exhaustion as it tries to decide which voice, command or suggestion to follow and how to respond to the welter of conflicting claims relentlessly made upon it. It is in an endless wobble between positive and negative seduction. The individual in a state of positive seduction abandons himself uncritically to a particular master or course of action. He believes that he will find security if he continues to cling to something stronger with blind devotion. He becomes a true believer in the one he deifies. He holds that one wholly responsible for his personal happiness and plans to move in on this benefactor as if he had found a rich uncle to be exploited.

But all situations rooted in leaning and depending on others result in disappointment. You can't feel let down unless you have been leaning on! Others refuse to carry us on their backs for long unless we *pay them well* for the ride. We are quickly dropped if we fail to make the situation profitable to those around us. The resulting disappointment becomes rage at the frequent frustrations, and this confuses the dependent mind. Out of an effort to retaliate, it becomes negatively dependent on others in the hope that it can escape its own habitual suggestibility. This results in what we commonly recognize as stubbornness, which makes the situation worse.

The negatively dependent individual wants to be independent but succeeds only in becoming a nay-sayer. He remains fully as suggestible as before and remains tied to the voice of outside authority as before—except that now he must do everything in reverse. Being contrary and contradicting others only breeds resistance in them and in us. All resistance only deepens our dependence on the thing we are resisting. Fighting only ties us to our enemy. To free ourselves, we must "let go" and "walk on."

Suggestibility deadens the mind and eventually destroys the ability to see and hear what is happening around us at the reality level. In Emerson's "Essay on Self-Reliance," he says:

> A man should learn to watch that gleam of light which flashes across his mind from within, more than the lustre of the firmament of bards and sages. Yet he dismisses without notice his thought, because it is his. In every work of genius we recognize our own rejected thoughts; they come back to us with a certain alienated majesty. Great works of art have no more affecting lesson for us than this. They teach us to abide by our own spontaneous impression with good-natured inflexibility then most when the whole cry of voices is on the other side. Else tomorrow a stranger will say with masterly good sense precisely what we have thought and felt all the time, and we shall be forced to take with shame our own opinion from another.

# 3 / *In the beginning*

Chart I pictures the position of a child at infancy. He is confronted by two worlds. There is the outside world of adults who are busy in the main tent of community living. They are busy creating the goods and services that are necessary if man is to survive on this earth. Each person has some role in this division of labor, since the task is too large for anyone to do entirely for and by himself. It is obvious that each task and each role demands some amount of training and willingness on the part of the one who does it. And some skills are more complex than others, thus demanding greater training and willingness to perform them.

The child at infancy neither knows nor cares about

# CHART I
# PATH TO MATURITY OR IMMATURITY

POINT B:
*Home*
The World of Enslavement
Arena of Dependency
Land of Special Privilege and Personal Recognition (Desire to be The Favored Child)
*Parents or Authority Figures*

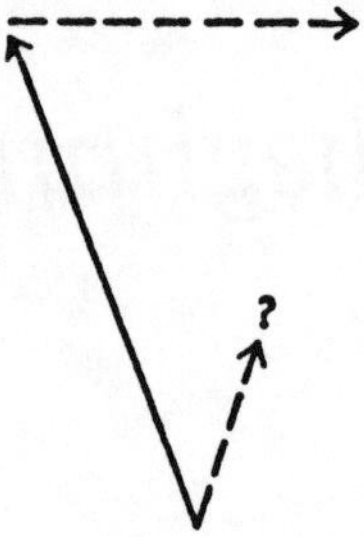


POINT C:
*The Outside World*
The Free World of Doing
The Impersonal World of Circumstance and Events
The What Is

POINT A:
*The Infant and Infantile Adult*

*The Child:*

- Depends on and clings to parents and other authority figures
- Has dominance-submission struggle against others by negative or positive means and strategies; competition for personal recognition (prestige)
- Tries manipulation and exploitation of people by positive and negative strategies
- Is a consumer of goods and services produced by others
- Escapes responsibility by putting own center-of-gravity onto others; negative-positive obedience (conformity); puts other heads higher than his own
- Has a begging attitude toward life (life owes him a living and happiness)
- Habitually "saves himself" at the expense of others; the withholding attitude toward life

*The Mature Adult*:

- Is Self-reliant
- Improvises solutions
- The job is his only boss and is the sole target of his attention
- Is non-attached and therefore non-competitive
- Is self-motivated in relation to confronting circumstances
- Manipulates the impersonal circumstances and things of life instead of manipulating people
- Is a producer of goods and services
- Has his center of gravity inside self
- Puts no head higher than his own
- Has a contributing, inventive attitude toward life
- Habitually "spends himself" in useful ways

this outside world. His immediate concern is the world of the home. He is helpless and has no other interest than to get nourishment for himself and satisfy his creature comforts. His helplessness makes him wholly dependent on what others give him and do for him. The big moments in his life are when someone *feeds or fondles him.* Getting or not getting is his main concern.

These moments of getting he enjoys and tries in various ways to increase their number. At a very early age, he finds that crying brings adults into his service when he is wet, hungry or bored. He also finds that smiling holds the attention of the adults who have the power to bring him benefits. He smiles when they pick him up and cries when they put him down. Thus each of us begins the basic habit of our life, the habit of manipulating people. We spend most of our childhood on the path from point A to point B developing our political skill in exerting influence over adults to get them to vote for us. And it is from this root that we have the neurotic acquisitive desire to make a good impression on others. It is at this point of our life that we get the idea that we must habitually lean and depend on the good opinion of others and fear their disapproval.

This path from point A to point B serves the needs of the child, but it *spells disaster* for us if we *continue in this way after we reach physical maturity.* The work of the outside world demands that each of us be self-reliant.

And the various functions of the mind as well as those of the body do not perfect themselves or come into focus unless we stand firmly on our own feet. No one can consider himself an adult, emotionally mature, as long as he seeks the outside world via the route from point A to point B to point C! Life demands that we go directly and spontaneously *on target* from point A to point C at all times. As adults we may no longer lean and depend on the opinions or the services of so-called authority figures for guidance, as we did when we were children. We must become both the doer and the deed!

All emotional failure arises from the fact that the individual is still trapped in the A-to-B-to-C approach to the solution of life's problems. No one can fail emotionally who has learned to go directly into the confronting situation. You can't feel let down if you haven't been *leaning on*! Neither a child nor a neurotic adult can hope to sustain himself on any kind of independent basis in this manner. Both are tied to the cradle, and each must live his life vicariously secondhand *through the activity* of another person.

The human animal is the only one prone to make this mistake and thus remain trapped in persisting infantilism. Nature puts her other animals on their own very shortly after birth. Kittens nurse greedily for weeks in the beginning as they are on the A-to-B development. But their tiny teeth begin to develop and get longer every day. Nursing her babies becomes painful to the mother in direct proportion to the length of the baby teeth. Her answer to that is to cut down gradually on the nursing time for her babies. Their efforts to persuade her to extend this time bear no fruit. All she does is to offer them solid food and in her own way suggest that they learn to go from A to C and stop bothering her for food. They resent her rejection of their dubious affection, and finally their hunger drives them independently to learn to eat solid food.

But the human animal spends approximately his first eighteen years leaning and depending on adults who continue to prop him up far more than is necessary for his welfare. Most parents continue to serve their children long, long after the children are old enough to do things for themselves. Civilization conspires to keep us on the path from A to B to C instead of liberating us. And thus it is that many are mistakenly encouraged to lean and depend and expect support from others *as if* they were still children.

The adult, then, must be consciously aware of any mental or physical habits he has that remain from his childhood and are keeping him in a subaltern, juvenile, dependent frame of mind. He must put away childish dependency.

# 4 / *After games, what?*

Perhaps this chapter ought to be entitled Thoughts on Leaving the Nest. Childhood has ended. During that period we were the center of almost constant attention and concern by our parents, teachers and others. Most of us had siblings with whom we were constantly involved, trying to maintain our pecking order to see that they did not get any advantages over us and that we lost none of our own. We were always under the shadow of some adult authority and there was never a time that we had our own *full initiative about anything*! Anything we decided was no more than a decision between Tweedledee and Tweedledum, since our parents had set the overall limits in the beginning. The thought of having freedom or having initiative as well *as full responsibility* for our activity was farthest from our mind!

Our life and its activities were structured and programmed, as Eric Berne calls the process, by parents, teachers, schools and other outside agents. We were free of responsibilities, and we either went along with parental demands or fought a delaying action as best we could. We were in almost total dependence on outside authority and had no reason to worry about being lonely or abandoned. But as childhood came to an end, we saw others going out into the world and knew we must soon begin to think and act for ourselves. Fear of having our own initiative and responsibility began to enter, and we were apt to feel blocked emotionally as to how we were going to enter this unknown adult world ahead of us. We were at a fork in the road, and there was seldom anyone to guide us as to which fork to take.

It is at this point that most of us make the fatal decision to continue on the path of conformity. In early life, we conformed either positively as good children or negatively as bad, delinquent children who did everything just in contrary reverse obedience. In both or either case, we were hanging on to one or the other end of the stick —*obedience.* Our dependence gave no other choice, of course. Our fear of the unknown is a strong force of inertia that tends to carry us along in the same old direction of conformity! Those who lacked anything to disrupt this inertia simply coasted or slid into physically adult life without being aware of the passage of time and found themselves housed in adult bodies—but with the same old dependency habits of a child! They were *unable to act with their own full initiative.* But life as an adult permits nothing less than full personal initiative of us.

Some estimates indicate that about 90% of the population lives in the stew of conformity. It is this lack of adult *initiative* that is at the root of our emotional problems. The question arises then as to how some of us escaped this common fate and why more of those who are now trapped do not escape into freedom?

Those who developed initiative in adolescence were fortunate in their choice of parents or surrogates when they were born. Adults who are themselves emotionally mature have free minds and do not play dominance-submission games with their children, so that their children have a chance to develop initiative. You have to start free to end free! So children of such parents have not learned to struggle against their parents and others for some useless dominance and are not interested in games of one-upmanship. Their transition from childhood to adult life is not a stormy series of defeats and struggles against outside authorities. It is a quiet growth in self-confidence in which they learn that there are few irremediable mistakes, and they regard a mistake as nothing more than a friendly invitation to keep trying—not a loss of love, approval and prestige, or as a humiliation to be avoided at any cost.

Those of us who have been caught in the net of conformity, however, have a wholly different picture of life, filled with struggle, fear, humiliation, envy and the endless hungry craving for personal recognition that never leaves us. Even when we are feeding it! And this presents us the answer to the second question! This eternal hunger for personal recognition, which is sometimes mistakenly called by a sick title, The Need for Love. *Exactly those* who most of all need to give up this infantile striving for outside recognition they call love are those who *find it most impossible to imagine enjoyment in anything apart from being the center of attention.* They fly like moths around a candle until they fly into the flame to end the torture of enslavement.

The habitually negatively obedient or positive conformist cannot imagine how he would structure, program or organize his daily activity if he did not depend on *outside initiative* to do it for him. As Eric Berne pointed out in his book *Games People Play,* most of our day is programmed for us by the necessity for sleep, getting up, going to work, doing a job, going to events, theaters, church, clubs or watching television. In all such activities, the initiative is in the hands of the outside agent, and we just go along for the ride until the undertaker comes. Then we hop on his wagon and go along with him to Boot Hill, as they say in the western. In truth, there isn't much time during day or evening when we have the need or opportunity to exercise full initiative on what we do with our energies. Most of our initiative is abdicated in the above situations, and we pretend that people in general are going to show the same parental warmth and eagerness to program and advance our welfare as our parents did when we were children. Alas for us!

But as adults, we may not abdicate our *initiative at any time.* Just as we would not lay down our pocketbook and not watch it while we do something else, we may not lay down our initiative and turn it over to someone else to exercise for us or in our default! We are born alone, we live alone and we die alone! No man can escape this fate. That *is exactly why we have been given this initiative,* so that we have something on which to depend—when we no longer have parents on whom to lean!

But the habitual conformist feels that *a life* in which he had to take full charge of his own initiative, and could not park it on some baby sitter or other parent substitute, *would be bleak, cold, lacking in interest and wholly unrewarding.* He is so dependent on expecting "goodies" from others as rewards for his behavior that he cannot imagine any independent life in which he is self-motivated and not dependent on someone else for his motivation and initiative.

It is exactly this angel with flaming sword who blocks the Eden of his dreams! He would love to be a hero and do independent, heroic deeds; but since no actor ever bothers to play to an empty house, he can't imagine doing it unless he is the center of attention and is guaranteed his reward. There has to be someone standing in the wings to pat him on the head and say, "Nice doggie" when he comes panting off the stage! As a child he had his parents, his siblings, his teachers. On the job he has the boss, his fellow workers, and at home his wife; he firmly believes they care and have nothing more rewarding to do for themselves than to keep watching to applaud his act. He counts on them to give him Brownie points or Green Stamps for his good deeds, and be emotional over his defeats! He lives in an emotional fog of wishful thinking that Big Brother (the boss) will single him out from all others for a reward and put his head higher than his siblings on the job!

The thought that he must give up this warm spicy brew of dreams, hopes, competition, anxiety, worry, fear, anticipation of Christmas or fear of defeat for the calm world—in which he would *use his own initiative* and not have to beg Brownie points or otherwise depend on the good opinion of others—seems as bleak and empty as an Arctic landscape. Not even a polar bear in sight or an igloo with smoke rising from the vent to cheer or motivate him to the release of initiative for himself.

He is so accustomed to the evils that grow out of dependence that he cannot imagine life without them. The fact that he labels them as threatening him with being cut off from those around him probably constitutes the basic reason why it is so difficult for him to give up his old way of life. This is obvious with alcoholics, drug addicts, gamblers and similarly trapped individuals. It isn't that they are so much in love with their addicting agent —liquor, drugs, horses—it is simply that they can't manage to live without the good or bad Brownie points they are accustomed to get from their pals who share the same addiction. Their whole social life is made up of others who have made the same conformist mistake, and they engage in constant sibling rivalry and the amusingly painful games of one-upmanship with these individuals. *Conformity is a way of life in which one can escape his own initiative and responsibility for creating his own happiness.* The conformists lean on Lady Luck or a mother substitute.

The objection made to the self-reliant approach outlined in this way of looking at life always boils down to the issue of how lonely one would be if he were emotionally independent. Such an individual cannot imagine how one would manage friendships, marriage and other close associations unless there are the customary immaturities, the abdication of initiative to another, the craving for personal recognition, pats on the head and other maternal rewards of obedient behavior. Before we can let go of our infantile habits and move onward to emotionally adult self-sufficiency, we must picture how we would achieve awareness, intimacy and spontaneity so we can enjoy the world around us and especially the company of the people next to us. But without having to *lean* on them!

People imagine that the self-sufficient person is aloof, cold, unsympathetic, disinterested and unfriendly toward those more dependent and less fortunate than he. But *exactly the contrary is true*. If this were not so, then there would indeed be no advantage to giving up playing infantile games of one-upmanship. The fact is that we cannot begin either to *enjoy our own inner capacities, association with others, or the world around us until and unless we have liberated ourselves from our leaning, dependent, derivative, enslaved, imitative, competitive, subaltern, childish habit of mind.* No self-respecting life can exist when we are attached and merely an appendage of someone else, since "when they take snuff we also have to sneeze." It is difficult to see how we can believe freedom is something to be avoided and believe that it would surely lead to loneliness and isolation.

Before we go further, then, let us picture in some detail how a person who has his own initiative acts and still enjoys fully and spontaneously the turmoil and variety of the whole life around him. In the first place, he is liberated from partiality and partisanship. If someone pipes a sad tune, he is not depressed by it and he does not have to dance along with the one who pipes it. Nor does he have to fight the feuds and hate the hates of others—just to be admitted to their circle and win approval or Green Stamps for his loyalty to their bias. He is free to be a friend to people regardless of whether or not they are on speaking terms with each other. Since he does not seek to win rewards from them, he has no fear that they can hurt him. It is only when *we seek benefits from others* that we fear or hate them. Only our dependent acquisitiveness spoils our relationships, when we approach our friends to get goodies from them and fear they may hold back on us.

When we are independently mature, our association with those around us will be free of any competitive attitude on our part. We will find no need to struggle for dominance and fear or resist submission. A person who approaches life with a self-reliant point of view puts no head higher than his own and therefore has no reason to be envious or obediently follow the heels of a pacemaker. Since he has no need to prove himself to anyone or to show off his personal superiority in order to win praise or admiration, he is like a good cardplayer who does not care what cards are dealt him since his fun lies in the free play he improvises in the playing of each hand. Each game is its own reward and he seeks nothing outside of the unfolding of each hand as it is played into the hands of others. He enjoys the whole experience and all that his partners do as well.

Awareness, intimacy and spontaneity can never be possible for us to experience so long as we are caught in the web of dependency, since "two is less than one," and we are inevitably dragged around by the twin we lean on! The kind of togetherness we endure is that of a hair shirt on our back—not the joy of freedom to ad-lib and be ourselves in the presence of other people, wherever we happen to be.

Only the free and equal can cooperate. It is obviously impossible for a master and a slave to cooperate with each other. Neither is free of the other, and the behavior of the one is strictly limited by the behavior of the other. There is no dominance-submission, superiority-inferiority, leader-follower or parent-child relationship based on dependence that does not deny and destroy personal initiative and prevent true cooperation from taking place. Since cooperation can take place only between equal partners, *neither of which has abdicated his own initiative* to the other, it is so rare that we seldom see it. But there is no relationship that is fit for a human being short of full cooperation. There is no such thing as a good master or a good slave.

What has too often passed as cooperation is a nauseating imitation of it called "togetherness," which is widely touted in novels and love songs. We are given to understand that we are nothing "until somebody loves us." Short of that, we can't hope to make the team. And to fail to make the team is the real fate worse than death! Nothing may be done unless it is on a team or in committee. Such unanimity obviously results in nonentity and total abdication of personal initiative. And it is equally obvious that it is the soil upon which political or emotional dictatorships grow. The free mind refuses to accept a single shred of such degrading subordination commonly called "reverence for higher-ups."

This does not mean at all that keeping your own initiative entitles you to a hard-nosed stubborn insistence on having your own way, come hell or high water. That would be obvious childishness and such inflexibility would defeat any person before he got far along his way. On the contrary, keeping your own initiative implies a flexible, inventive, quiet persistence in exploring and creating until everything that needs to be done is accomplished. In Great Britain, the party out of power is called the "loyal opposition," and it is expected to develop *its own views* of how the country can be run! It must be prepared at any moment to step in and do a complete job if the other party in power fails to function. It may not rightly use its power only to block and embarrass the incumbents in a kind of negative obedience. It has a responsibility to invent new and better answers to current problems, just as if it were currently in charge of the country. That is democracy in action, and in it there is no room for abdication of initiative, imitative competition or sabotage of others currently in power.

Cooperation is a joyous affirmation of the full initiative of oneself and also that of every other person. Jimmy Durante is quoted as saying, "Let everyone the hell alone." You certainly do not always have to be in unison to cooperate. Since cooperation is such a misunderstood term, perhaps we can spell out how it sometimes operates at the level of daily contacts.

The most common kind of cooperation is that which exists between the butcher, baker and candlestick maker. Each has his own function and his own know-how to do it. Their hours are different and the operations are not the same. Each function is equally important to society. Each elaborates his own function according to his imagination as best he can. They may not know, or feel personally attracted or friendly to, each other for that matter. Liking the other person is not basic to cooperation with him. But each is fully responsible for the excellence of his own product, and he fulfills himself in producing it. Each is cooperating with all the others, since he eventually *exchanges goods for goods with them as they do with him.*

Another kind of cooperation is possible as with oarsmen who stroke in unison to accomplish their tasks. Each pulls equally and with exact timing to each other to be effective. To accomplish this kind of timing each has to have his own *inner consent and full initiative.* He does not feel dominated, obedient or a second-class citizen. Here again, the participants do not have to like each other on any personal basis. That is irrelevant to releasing his own energies, as he is not dependent on them for approval.

It is probable that most people mistake, or at least confuse, conformity with cooperation or do not have a clear enough picture to tell them apart. We must not expect everyone to march to the same drumbeat. Conformity is mutual enslavement. Cooperation is *mutual liberation* and freedom.

Doing things together may or may not be cooperation, depending on whether each *maintains his own initiative throughout.* The baker sets his dough at night and has to have his rolls ready for the table by breakfast time so that the butcher and candlestick maker can go about their separate trades. They certainly do not have to help each other, and any attempt to do so would only result in each getting into the way of the other. But each is certainly responsible to make sure that nothing *encroaches on his own peck rights* so that he is not obstructed in the fulfillment of his job. *He has to satisfy the needs of his own life—first!* It is not his job to please others first! And then use that as an excuse to neglect his own production.

We please others best—and best satisfy ourselves—

only when we have *done our own job fully* and thus *fulfilled* our own potential. We destroy ourselves and serve others least when we go along weakly with their schemes in a pretense or pretext of cooperation. All are cheated by that approach. Such going along leaves us feeling deprived and unfulfilled without enriching others.

In other words, cooperation is only the free activity engaged in by equal adults, each of whom has kept his personal initiative and seeks no reward from the other. It is *never similar to mutual enslavement.* Its end result is greater individual self-realization; it does not diminish either person by any form of crippling. It is never cooperation unless each of us is *working on his own*—but not in a way that denies the same kind of initiative to the others.

It should be evident now that there is no trace of loneliness or isolation facing the person who gives up playing dependency games of mutual enslavement and learns to stand alone. And it is equally evident that fun and the real enjoyment in life only begins when he is able to give up the restrictive subordinating bounds of childhood and engage in freely cooperative activities with the real things, people and circumstances. The person who is crippled by the infantile games he plays can only go as far as such games allow him to go in life. It is useless to send a boy to do a man's work. A man's work cannot be done by anyone—unless he has freedom with its full awareness, intimacy and spontaneity.

And as far as the greatest of all fears is concerned—the fear of loneliness—we are only able to be free of this fear, once and for all time, if we find our own center-of-gravity and personal initiative. Aloneness is freedom-from-dependence! Loneliness, on the other hand, is the dependent lost child crying as it searches for the parent or baby-sitter it has lost and cannot find.

If it is fully understood that self-reliance is a starting point, as well as middle and end point, for our life, and that anything less than full personal initiative is the source of all our pain, then we can continue to explore in further chapters the nature of those mistakes that hinder us from choosing self-reliance as our way-of-life.

Each of us, then, is faced with making a conscious decision whether he will choose the mutually-manipulative way-of-life characteristic of the child and the emotionally immature adult, or whether he will decide to discover the nonmanipulative approach that opens up . . . *after we give up playing games with each other.*

# 5 / *Life on the grazing principle*

The person who sees life as a competition and the world as a competitive place is astonished when anyone suggests that the world is not a competitive place, but that there are many competitive people who make it appear that way to those who are themselves competitive. Reality is what it is and in itself is neither competitive nor noncompetitive.

But if they do try to accept this statement, they find themselves unable to visualize the world on any other than a competitive basis. More than that, they cannot imagine how anyone would function in a noncompetitive world. How would he behave and what would he use for motivation if he did not pursue the competitive ideal and the myth of success? He can think of nothing to give life substance, purpose, meaning or direction. He can think of no satisfying reason why anyone would do anything at all unless some reward is held out to him by someone. The idea that the fun lies in the doing and the action is its own reward is quite beyond his comprehension. In fact, the picture of a world without competition does not interest him.

But in truth, a competitive approach to life narrows our whole view of life and the world. It blinds us to anything outside the narrow goals we set for ourselves. Competition is conformity to a pattern, and conformity breeds stupidity, narrowness, bigotry, idolatry and other forms of exclusiveness. This explains why a highly ambitious person seems to be a self-centered bore who has only a superficial contact with life around him. He has a hypersensitive ego and his pride or vanity is easily hurt. But he is, in reality, quite dull and insensitive to anything apart from the main chance he hopes to exploit to achieve his goal. And when his goal is reached, he finds himself at a sudden loss to know what to do next or what further direction he should follow.

The self-reliant person who is not trapped in competitive games of one-upmanship and enslaved by playing useless games of mutual manipulation does not face this stultifying dead end in life. He has learned to live his life on the Grazing Principle, without set, compulsive goals to follow or outside authority figures to obey and placate. He follows a much deeper law which operates without any effort of will on his part. It is the law of the inner gleam, or spirit, and it operates without his having to take thought or make it work. It is as automatic as swallowing. Adler used to say, "If you had to have a rule for swallowing, you would choke to death."

The Grazing Principle is at the root of all the great discoveries, and it is the path of our enlightenment. It might be called "horse sense," since every horse is a fine exponent of the principle. If you turn him loose on a roadside, he begins to graze immediately. He sees a clump of grass and starts to eat. While he is nibbling this clump, he sees another not more than a half-step away. He reaches for it and, as he is cropping it, his eye falls on still another clump just a short step ahead of him. And that is all he does all day! But by nightfall, he is miles away from where he started. Without any thought of "getting ahead in life," he has moved into new grazing areas continuously. And most of all, he has enjoyed every minute of the process. No fuss or anxiety. No need for rewards or recognition from outside himself. His moment-to-moment fulfillment has been its own reward, and he has no dependence on anything at the end of the day to pay him for his effort. He does not live on the deferred-payment plan but remains in the here-and-now throughout the whole day. And not once does he abandon his own initiative in the process.

Human beings have so exaggerated the importance of their forebrain, with its planning power and critical faculties—that thing we call the intellect—that they cannot imagine it is possible for a person to live on the Grazing Principle. But as a matter of fact, some things cannot be accomplished on any other plan. The person who is truly an innovator, or creator, in any art or science must depend wholly on the Grazing Principle to lead him into new pastures and discoveries. The conscious, planning intellect is quite powerless to free itself from conditioning of the past. It cannot escape old habits of thought and cross into the Promised Land itself. If we do not trust the Grazing Principle in us—our intuition—we cannot do anything except shuttle back and forth within the limits of the safe old formulas of the past.

Since we habitually live almost exclusively on the intellect and have been trained to mistrust our inner gleam, as Emerson calls it, we believe that the Grazing Principle does not exist or has been lost in man. Fortunately, it is quite alive in those few areas where we dare to let it work for us. Surprising as it may seem, we exercise it three times a day at the dinner table when we eat. We go grazing when we let our fork take over, have a mind of its own and feed us as it wills. We face no quandaries deciding which bite to pick up first. No one has a breakdown trying to decide whether to have two bites of potatoes before a bite of meat, to be followed by a nibble on the string beans, then to be followed by a sip of coffee. It all just happens. Our fork knows exactly where to go, how much to pick up and where it will go for the next bite. It wanders aimlessly over the plate and before we know it the plate is empty and we are ready for second helpings. And we did the whole enjoyable process entirely without conscious deliberation, using only the Grazing Principle.

The self-reliant person, who is nonobedient and nonsubmissive to conformity, old habits and the worship of authorities, lives each day in this condition of spontaneous awareness. His intimacy with the existing moment keeps him in a state of discovery. Each moment is new and never repeats itself, regardless of what seemingly monotonous job he may be doing.

Those who dare not trust themselves to be totally self-dependent in their approach protest loudly that their life in the home, or on the job making a living under the iron heel of their boss, does not allow them to exercise the Grazing Principle. This is, of course, only an alibi to avoid facing their leaning, dependent, irresponsibly obedient escapist and conformist way of approaching and doing things. We might accept their complaints seriously and believe their boss and job prevented them—if we found them *on the Grazing Principle in their leisure time!* This is exactly the spot where they betray *their dependence at its worst!* Though they are free to exercise full initiative, they seek someone else to plan their day for them. They are wholly dependent in the way they spend their leisure time.

The structuring of leisure time is one of the most stringent and revealing tests of our ability to hold up our own pants and maintain our own initiative and identity. The gross inability of many of us to program, structure, organize or fill our own time is often masked by television, chores set by others, our job, rituals and customs of the community which keep us busy without calling on our own ability. But when we finally face the leisure for the self-expression we say we want, most of us are at a total loss unless we can find someone who will take us by our moist, sticky hands and let us go tagging along with them. For most people, leisure time is spelled L-O-N-E-L-I-N-E-S-S! They are totally incapable of grazing their way through an hour, a day or a lifetime. They cannot do with their own initiative as well as their fork does for them at feeding time.

Newton was just sitting—doing nothing—under a tree when he saw an apple fall. He was being quiet for a while. Nothing new about a falling apple; he had seen a thousand fall before! But the Grazing Principle happened to be around, and it wandered by just then. It informed him that he had just discovered the law of gravity! All the really new discoveries enter this world in this manner—on the Grazing Principle. The anxiety-ridden, ambitious turbulence of the conscious mind makes grazing quite out of the question. We can't have it both ways; we must choose.

# 6 / *Competition*

Competition enslaves and degrades the mind. It is one of the most prevalent and certainly the most destructive of all the many forms of psychological dependence. Eventually, if not overcome, it produces a dull, imitative, insensitive, mediocre, burned-out, stereotyped individual who is devoid of initiative, imagination, originality and spontaneity. He is humanly dead. Competition produces zombies! Nonentities!

Competition is a process or variety of habitual behavior that grows out of a habit of mind. It originates from our need to imitate others during early childhood. But it is a sign of persisting infantilism if it is still dominating us after adolescence. It is a sign of retarded psychological development, a persisting childishness of "Monkey see—monkey do." We are trapped in imitation.

Once established in orbit, as an habitual way of looking at interpersonal relationships, it contaminates all our relationships. It becomes a way of relating to the world, to other people and to confronting situations. Competition is a *killer* because it deprives the individual of personal initiative and responsibility.

The habit of competing is so widespread that many people firmly believe that it is a law of nature. Competition is frequently praised as a great virtue to be developed by everyone. This is a costly misunderstanding, since human skills develop adequately only in cooperation, a condition of reinforcement. Competition always lies at cross-purposes with cooperation and thus frustrates individual human initiative.

This unfortunate misunderstanding arises from the fact that people seem to see a superficial resemblance between initiative and competition. Many even regard them as identical like mistaking toadstools for mushrooms. Unless we clearly see the difference between the two, we cannot hope to avoid the evils attendant on competition. It tries in every way to imitate initiative. But the sad reality remains: we compete with others only in those situations *in which we are afraid and defective in initiative.* Those who can, do! Those who cannot, or dare not, imitate!

Initiative is the most highly prized of virtues. It is a vital necessity for everyone, since all human problems demand activity. Human problems do not get solved *where personal initiative* is lacking. Self-reliance is not possible without initiative, and one cannot fulfill his own potentialities unless he is both emotionally and physically self-reliant. *Nothing can take the place of personal initiative* in the life of an individual. It is for this reason that we place such high value on initiative and on the individual who has developed it.

Initiative is the opposite of competition, and *one is the death of the other.* Initiative is a natural quality of a *free mind.* It is wholly spontaneous and intuitive in its response to confronting situations as they arise, like the thrusts of a swordsman. The free mind allows one to be an *inner-directed* person whose responses in action are automatic. Competition, on the contrary, is merely an *imitative response* that *lags behind* while it *waits* for its direction from someone whose head appears to us to be taller and who has been chosen by us to set the pace and direction of our activity. In short, initiative produces spontaneous action, whereas competition produces only delayed *reaction* to stimuli from a pacemaker!

Competition grows out of dependence. It imitates initiative in a deceptive way and thus clouds our understanding. The competitive individual trains himself to outrun his pacemaker, and we may imagine from the result that he is enjoying the fruits of initiative. He often develops much skill so that he appears masterful and competent. As a result of his success, he is often put in a key position where he must originate and organize policy in an unstructured situation that demands independent, imaginative, original planning or activity. In such situations, he cannot function inventively, since he has trained himself only to outrun or imitate *existing patterns*; he has no freedom of mind to create or improvise new forms. He spends his working days in a bind or trap.

To free the mind from the habit of competition, we must see in detail the process by which the mind is ensnared by competition. The way out of a trap is to know the way the trap is built. Only then will it cease being a trap. The release from the stranglehold of competition lies in the increase of self-reliance, since competition can only arise out of a lack of self-reliance! It is that simple. Self-dependence accomplishes that which competition can never touch.

As we have said, the competitive person makes pacemakers out of those he sees around him and puts their heads higher than his own. He abdicates his own birthright doing so. Having abdicated his own initiative, he then begins the struggle to surpass those *he places higher* than himself. Thus he grows blind to his own inner potentialities and, in time, is fully under the hypnotic influence of his self-elected pacemakers. He feels hypnotized by them. He enters into a condition of total dependence on outside direction in the sense that he uses others as if they were seeing-eye dogs to guide him. He dares not use his own intuition or spontaneity. Thus, he is in a state of continual irresponsibility, exercising no mind of his own and merely reacting to others. If they take snuff, it is he who sneezes.

An old Zen monk, named Rinzai, summarized his impatience with such individuals by saying:

> If on your way you meet the Buddha, kill him. . . . O disciples of the truth, make an effort to free yourselves from every object. . . . O you, with eyes of moles! I say to you: No Buddha, no teaching, no discipine! What are you ceaselessly looking for in your neighbor's house? Don't you understand that you are putting a head higher than your own? What then is lacking to you in yourselves? That which you have at this moment does not differ from that of which the Buddha is made.

It is evident that the habit of competition is based on, or linked to, another habit—of *making comparisons!* We compare ourselves as either above or below others. We fear those we fancy are below us lest they somehow displace us in an effort to get above us. Thus life appears to us as just one big, dangerous game of one-upmanship in which we always stand amidst enemies against whom we must somehow rise and triumph. Or so we imagine it to be.

The built-in hell of the competitive person is that he stamps himself in his own mind as second-class, lacking initiative and originality. A follower! It is exactly that feeling which relentlessly drives him to compete. The self-reliant person feels no desire to compete or otherwise prove himself, either to himself or to others. In short, all competition is second-class or derivative behavior; a back without a brain, incapable of finding its own way or choosing its own objective. It must lean and depend on the pacemaker of its own envious selection.

Comparison breeds fear, and fear breeds competition and one-upmanship. We believe our safety depends on killing off the one above us by outrunning him at his own game. We have no time to enjoy any game of our own making lest we lose ground in our race against others for status and preferment. And we may not rest lest those below us steal ahead in the night when we are not aware. The higher we rise, the greater will be our fear of falling. And so we are fearful regardless of *whether we win or lose* the daily skirmishes.

This type of hypnosis is a form of monomania in which one subordinates himself to the commands of someone he accepts as an authority figure. In short, our total dependence on him leads us to total ignoring of all other signals from our environment. *We lose the ability to see and hear* that which is plainly visible around us. We cling to the traditional forms of the game he induces us to play. We thereby sacrifice all of our inborn ability to respond spontaneously to the confronting realities of life. We can see, hear or respond only *vicariously* through the eyes and judgments of the pacemaker whom we imitate or obey. This loss of ability—to see, hear or respond to emerging reality—*is the most damaging factor* of competition and its wasteful, dominance-submission struggle.

The desire for preferment above others and for personal status leads to the degrading dependence on the opinion of other people and a *pathetic craving for words of praise from them.* The desire for praise carries with it a terror lest others disapprove. Thus the mind is enslaved by the craving for the good opinion of those around us. And so, one can say that the need for personal recognition is merely childish.

The ambitious, competitive individual, then, is an unfortunate who is still trapped in the childhood desire to become the favored child. He stands with his begging bowl before others and pleads for their approval. He will run, jump, steal, lie, murder or do anything he feels is necessary to do in order to win the praise he seeks. He must somehow impress and thus possess the head that he puts above his own. Since he still views life as a child or as a second-class citizen, all his efforts to get ahead only serve to confirm his habitual way of regarding others and tie him to them. He continues on this path until someone can help him to break the hypnotic spell that binds him by showing him what he has been, and is, doing.

One of the basic, emotional attitudes that underlie competition is the feeling of hostility; there is no such thing as friendly competition. All competition is hostile. It grows out of a desire to achieve a position of dominance and to enforce submission over others. The desire for dominance, in turn, arises from a desire to use and exploit the other person, either psychologically or physically.

This desire to exploit others puts us at cross-purposes with others. We disrupt cooperation and disturb others by either active or passive means. We insist on changing the rules of the game to put them at a disadvantage and to give us a preferred position. We are easily irritated if things happen in any way but the way we want them. Those we cannot find use for appear only as boring, and we want to ignore or belittle them. We feel comfortable with others only when we have a favorable situation and others look up to us.

The competitive individual is always a poor sport. He cannot stand any situation long in which he is not ahead of others. If he feels he cannot win, he becomes a spoil-sport and wants to ruin the game for others. Or he loses courage and interest in the game, so that he retires from it. Or he will only play those games of function in those situations in which he stands a good chance of dominating.

The spirit of competition is the opposite of the spirit of play. The competitive person is incapable of play for the sake of play because he must win or make a good impression. This is easy to see with those who play cards. The competitive cardplayer always wants to win. He groans or is in misery if he is given a bad hand in a deal. He becomes bitter and filled with self-pity every time he loses a trick and blames others for his bad luck. If he gets a good hand, he gloats in a superior way and tries to make others envious of his good fortune. For him, the whole game is only an exercise in hate; he will cheat to win if he dares. With him, winning, not playing, is all that counts.

It has been said that the world is divided into haters and creators. Watching people play cards makes this easy to see. The competitive player in cards—or, in the game of life—has no joy. He lives in fear that he will be put down. But the emotionally self-reliant person plays cards in the "spirit of the picnic." There is no such thing as a bad hand to him, because he does not care whether he wins or loses in the game. The process of playing is his joy. One hand is just as interesting to him as another, since none is like the other. His pleasure is to see exactly what fascinating patterns emerge as the game is played and where he can fit his cards into this changing, developing flux of circumstance. He plays intuitively and without any fear at all, since he is free of any need to win or lose. His whole mind is free to enjoy whatever happens, and he can take any risks he likes with his plays or follow any hunch he may have as to how to play his hand. His only goal is to see what happens—to explore and discover potentialities, not to prove himself.

In summary, the competitive person operates out of constant fear. Fear always limits and degrades us. We can never achieve our potential ability in the climate of fear that competition breeds. Dependence leads to fear; fear leads to comparisons; comparisons lead to competition, and competition eventually destroys us by degrading us to imitation, conformity, infantilism or mediocrity. Dependence and imitation never lead to creativity and independence. Freedom comes only when we put no head higher than our own.

Chart II, The Desire for Personal Recognition, is a pictorial summary of competition. In this chart, it is important to understand that envy is the Siamese-twin of competition; they are never found separate and apart. One is the shadow cast by the other. The basic difference is that envy is the name we give to dependence at the *emotional* level, and competition is the term we use to

# CHART II
# THE DESIRE FOR PERSONAL RECOGNITION

- *I seek preferment, please love me*
- *Making "love affairs" out of personal and business relationhips*

LEADS TO:

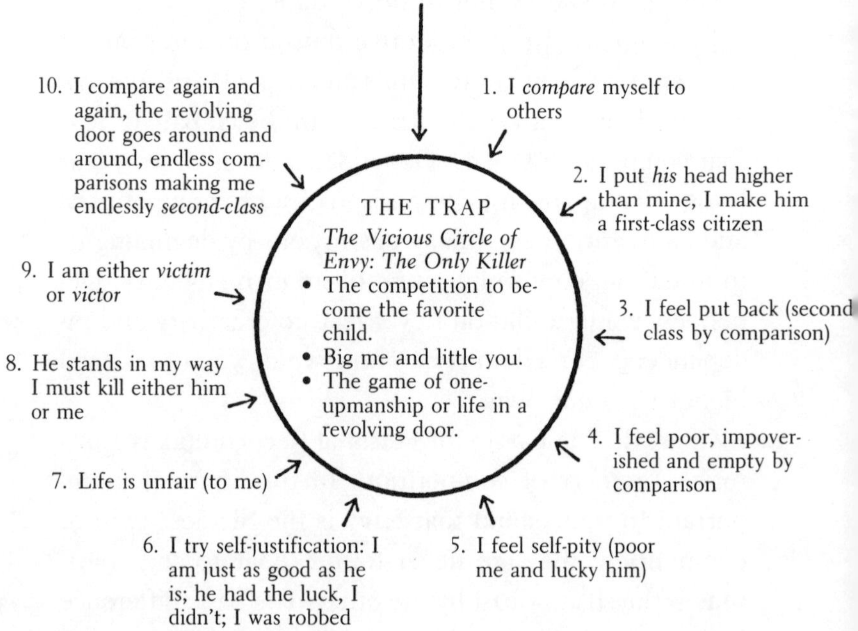
1. I *compare* myself to others
2. I put *his* head higher than mine, I make him a first-class citizen
3. I feel put back (second class by comparison)
4. I feel poor, impoverished and empty by comparison
5. I feel self-pity (poor me and lucky him)
6. I try self-justification: I am just as good as he is; he had the luck, I didn't; I was robbed
7. Life is unfair (to me)
8. He stands in my way I must kill either him or me
9. I am either *victim* or *victor*
10. I compare again and again, the revolving door goes around and around, endless comparisons making me endlessly *second-class*
THE TRAP
*The Vicious Circle of Envy: The Only Killer*
• The competition to become the favorite child.
• Big me and little you.
• The game of one-upmanship or life in a revolving door.

describe the result of dependent behavior that accompanies it at the *action* level. What is true of one is exactly true of the other—just as the image in a mirror exactly reflects the behavior of the object in front of it. Or, one could say, that envy is emotion, and emotions are only the steam we must generate to carry out our purposes; all action demands energy, and emotion supplies us the power we need. Thus it is that competition and envy are parallel action-feeling.

# 7 / *The double bind*

The Double Bind is the situation that happens when the wishful behavior of the immature individual runs into the implacable demands of the reality of the here-and-now! As we have shown, the child is habitually putting other heads higher than his own. *And so does the immature individual*; that is what shows that he is immature. He pictures such individuals as authority figures who must be manipulated by him to achieve his wishes. He regards them as his bosses who must be obeyed. As long as one is a child, he has only to satisfy the expectations of such figures.

An adult has no such easy time of things. He is faced with the reality of the outside world. It demands that he be a help and no longer a burden. He is expected to operate in the world outside the home and become a producer of goods and services. He finds that he is expected to produce these values and offer them in exchange for the benefits he seeks from others. To his dismay, he finds that nothing is granted freely without cost to him, as when he was a child. Now he must pay for what he wants. And if his product is small, he can expect only a small return for it. He finds himself in an *impersonal world* which is not at all moved by his smiles or his tears. Nor is it impressed *whether he likes* his situation or not. And then he finds that manipulating people *no longer solves his problems for him.*

In short, The Job Is the Only Boss. The job is that particular bit of reality we face *right in front of us* at any given time. It is always demanding something of us, and it refuses to go away if we ignore it. Nothing but impersonal handling resolves the situation for us. If we try to escape from it by a detour through some other person, it turns up immediately in some other spot to block us.

Thus the immature individual is trapped between serving two masters. Or, as Alfred Adler described it, "trying to chase two rabbits at once and catching neither." His whole past conditioning has left him with no ability to go directly "on target" in an impersonal attempt to meet the demands that confront him in the situation. But he must face *the job* and appear to be making an effort to solve the problem. He looks at it with half an eye. But the other eye is casting wildly about to see if he can find someone he can press, impress or influence either into getting him *excused* from serving the job or to *do it for him* in his place.

The Double Bind is the point at which the impact of past habit comes into conflict with the demands of the here-and-now, and all immaturities are immediately exposed as *inferiorities.* The feeling of inferiority is the anticipation of such defeats as one knows must happen in that event. The individual takes a step forward toward the problem and a step backward away from it, thus standing at the same spot. He seems to vibrate and dither in his quandary. It is as if he were driving a car, and the red-and-green traffic signals were both burning at the same time. He is getting signals to hold back and signals to go forward simultaneously. Obviously he can bring himself to do neither.

This Double Bind is the core of every human *emotional* problem. The job demands a clear mind that is *not subordinated to outside authority.* The free mind goes directly on target as an arrow. It is not caught in the gravitational field of some other person; it has no need to deviate and manipulate someone. It has the quality of "aloneness" which we see as singleness of purpose—as full initiative.

Failure, then, results from this unfortunate split in the

attention of an individual. His old conditioning leads him to seek the master he loves to lean on the most; he looks fearfuly about in his ambition for personal recognition. He must find a way to seem to be a big shot and thus avoid the task.

It is the ambition to be a big shot that brings an *equivalent fear—of falling* down! The higher one aspires, the farther one has to fall and the greater the *fear* to *move*. Thus the Double Bind is compounded of equal parts of greed and caution. The immature person will give us neither his ambition for approval nor his fear of disapproval. The desire to manipulate, impress and exploit has the fear of failing built into the core. As it says in the Bible, the coward flees even when no man pursues. We not only fear we may not be able to make a good impression (exploit); we also fear the situation in which we may be tested.

Stage fright is an excellent example of being trapped in the Double Bind. A person who is dependent on the good opinion of those around him fears making a speech; he is afraid that he will not impress the audience favorably and they will not love him. He prepares his speech and finds he is able to do it without faltering at home or before his family. But when he stands before his audience, it suddenly goes out of his mind and he cannot recall a word of it. He merely stands and trembles.

It is obvious to us what has happened. He didn't really

want to make the speech in the first place as it represented a possible loss of esteem if he did not make a big impression. He merely wanted attention. When he finally faced the sea of strange faces, his full attention flew to the *pursuit of his favorite rabbit*; his desire to make a good impression and win personal recognition. Thus his mind is a blank as far as the content of his speech is concerned. He has no psychic energy available to put on the task he came to do—to make a speech.

It is most important for us to remember something each of us knows but is apt to forget: the mind cannot *pursue two targets simultaneously*! The mind behaves much like an electric circuit in that it is either *on* or it is *off*. There is no halfway with us; it is either *yes* or *no*. We often say, "Yes . . . but. . . . " And this always means no!

It is this neurological factor that causes the block, of course. The dither that happens is the effort of the mind to zigzag back and forth between the two rabbits. The individual feels that he may not ignore either objective, as he sees the situation; so the best he can do is to hop back and forth with his attention, which becomes hopelessly split and dissipated.

The mind is like the body in that it works automatically and without pain unless we are making some mistake. We do not know we have a stomach or a foot if all is going well with them. Nor do we have any self-consciousness or emotional anguish if we are not trapped in some mistaken certainty. The function of pain is the same for both the mind and body; it tells us when we are not living rightly. And, when we stop to look at emotional pain, we will always find the Double Bind.

## CHART III
## THE FALL OF A MAN ARISES FROM EMOTIONAL DEPENDENCE*

| *Free Mind: Active-Productive* | *Enslaved Mind: Passive-Receptive* |
|---|---|
| Creates | Seeks to "become as a God"<br>Be a "big shot" |
| Gives | Takes |
| Initiates | Has begging attitude:<br>"Please love me"<br>Conforms<br>Makes envious comparisons |
| Ad-libs | Has leader-follower illusion |
| Is nonattached | Is suggestible:<br>Positive-negative<br>Feels put back<br>Seeks moral support<br>Begs personal recognition |
| Has no desire to impress | Desires to impress<br>Great expectations<br>Leans on opinion of others<br>Superiority-inferiority feelings |
| Has center-of-gravity inside | Has center-of-gravity in others |
| Has spontaneous activity | Follows rules in cookbook |
| Improvises | Imitates |
| Sees reality | Sees appearances |

* *Emotional Dependence is the craving for recognition above others—the desire to dominate, to impress, to influence, to exploit—and leads to "The Double Bind" or "Chasing Two Rabbits at Once" (See Chart IV).*

# CHART IV
# THE DOUBLE BIND:
# CHASING TWO RABBITS AT ONCE

*Full Attention:*
*Creative Power = 100%*

*Formula:*
*Full Attention = 100%*
*(Creative Power)*
*Subtract Need for Personal Recognition*
*Remainder = Available Attention to Give the Job!*
*F.A. minus P.R. = % for Job*

*The Job*
*(The Confronting Reality of the Here and Now)*

The Job Is the Only Boss. It is the confronting moment of the Now that must have my undivided attention. The Job is that confronting demand of Reality which must be met and manipulated. It determines what I must do and how it can be done.

My life is the way I habitually meet this situation. My mind should be free of outside demands so as to be fully available to the demands of the Now!

*The Free Mind*

The Free Mind is unstructured and without forms, convictions, ideas, conclusions, bias, conditioning, attachments, judgments, ideals, hopes, likes, dislikes, reverence, obedience or any other precondition. It is similar to water in that it can flow into and around everything regardless of shape or size; it fits into anything.

*The Craving for Personal Recognition*
*(The Desire to Be the Favored Individual)*

Other people become the boss. They become parent figures in my imagination, and I seek to manipulate them for my advantage. I must beg or struggle with them to get my way and what I must have. They, not the Job, become my control.

The Begging Attitude is the passive-receptive attitude of the immature child, or the "Please love me" approach to others.

The craving for power to rule and dominate others, or the desire to enslave and exploit others for personal gain, is part of this picture.

An aspect of the Begging Attitude is the Enslaved Mind—enslaved by wishful thinking. The world of wishes or ideal solutions is the world of the child.

It acts spontaneously without any effort of will by us. It responds in a flash without our "taking thought" and meets problems in unstructured ways (original). It ad-libs answers to problems in an inspired way. The Mind (Spirit) refuses to be enslaved by our own wishes or the command of others. As Spirit, it behaves as the wind which "bloweth where it listeth, and thou hearest the sound thereof but canst not tell whence it cometh, and whither it goeth."

The Free Mind manipulates circumstance and things, *not people*. It refuses to crowd itself into old forms, traditions, customs, conditioning. It deals instantly with confronting problems without hesitating for deliberation. (The first guess is probably inspired and, intuitively, the best one.)

The center-of-gravity lies within itself; never in outside authority ("Be a lamp unto your own feet"). Puts no head higher than itself; maintains first-class citizenship vis-à-vis all others.

Matter-of-fact, live-and-let-live relationships with others. Is nonjudgmental. It makes no invidious comparisons, beliefs or value systems for itself. Views reality unedited and unlimited.

*The Enslaved Mind*

The Enslaved Mind leans on crutches of praise or blame, seeks approval and shuns blame.

Leans on the opinion of others, tries to manipulate others by creating a good impression.

In hypnotic obedience (suggestibility) to others. Negative-positive reactivity to the control of others. Either submissive or stubbornly negative. Allergic to people.

Puts other heads higher than own. Feels self as a second-class citizen. Habitually makes invidious comparisons. Feels either superior or inferior as a result.

Hypersensitive feelings. Easily hurt and feels others should protect his feelings and welfare. Makes them responsible for his unhappiness.

Competes habitually for status—to be one-up on others. Rivalry traps him in endless envy and feelings of being deprived. Habitually has the feeling of poverty.

Fear of failure. Seeks rewards and assurances from others. Habitually withholds self (saves self) in search of the illusion of security. Wants others to protect him. Seeks special privilege.

*Note*: When the craving for recognition is greater than the desire to do the Job, then it is done inadequately and we fail. The result: the individual fails to win the recognition he seeks and he fails the Job. Thus he loses both rabbits.

Charts III and IV represent the elements of the Double Bind. It is evident why the mind cannot satisfy these simultaneous demands and how we end up one or the other, the free mind or the enslaved mind. We have a choice. We must give up all dependence on outside authority figures and be willing to walk alone; the way out of the fire is through the middle! Only an increase in self-reliance can release the Double Bind. We must let go and walk on, leaving the unresolved dependencies and traditions, the likes and dislikes of childhood behind us as we go.

# 8 / *The rebellious habit of mind*

There is, perhaps, no worse misfortune than to develop the rebellious habit of mind! And no person to be pitied more than the rebellious person. And no one so self-deceived as a person who is a habitual nay-sayer in the belief that he is expressing a mind and individuality of his own. The humiliating aspect of it is that he imagines that he is being original in his endless opposition, whereas he is only being the other end of the stick—not his own free agent. He spits defiantly into the wind, in the belief that if he keeps on doing it, he will eventually manage to make it go where he intends and not fly back into his face. The catastrophe lies in the fact that a rebel may often destroy himself in such senseless resistance and never realize that he is fighting absolutely no one but himself.

Dependence usually expresses itself in positive conformity, submission, obedience. Most people are eager to obey and thus escape all personal responsibility. But dependence can just as easily express itself as negative conformity in blind disobedience. Such contrariness is very attractive to some individuals, since it is often mistaken for self-reliance, independence, initiative! The rebel certainly fancies himself as a strong character, 100% self-determined, a free mind and a free spirit who is acting wholly on his own. He cannot be reached in his understanding because of this self-deception. This explains why neither punishment nor kindness has any effect on the criminal, the addict and similar delinquent, the alcoholic. Rebellious individuals are, in fact, caught on both sides of the coin of conformity; both negative and positive. They are in positive obedience to the code of their gang and in negative obedience to the pressures of the community! Thus they have nothing that resembles independence, self-reliance, a mind of their own.

The rebel is under a kind of hypnotic illusion in which he sees himself a white knight on horseback fighting dragons. Thus rebels are able to hide their timidity, fearfulness, dependence on the opinion of others *from their own awareness*! The more their situation worsens, the more they toughen their habitual negativity and thicken their skins to create a deadlock! The irresistible force and the immovable object come together. If a rebel ever had any inkling of a mind of his own, it seems to disappear. He remains abysmally negatively obedient to external pressures right up to his own destruction. In short, the rebel is a living stalemate, in total dependence on the outside environment and unable to pull out of the trance-like state in which he finds himself.

It is easier to understand such negative obedience if we see that these efforts the rebel is making are those of a child who wants to be a show-off and win the approval of the parent but has failed to get the desired attention. In resentment and discouragement, he finds that he can get their reluctant attention just as well, or even better, if he gives them the hotfoot when they do not look at him.

The average person is addicted to positive approval and cannot understand the lengths to which these others go just to be noticed. Any kind of notoriety is preferred by them to being overlooked. Criminals often clip press notices of their exploits and proudly treasure them as if they had made contributions on the useful side of life. Their feeling of insignificance is so vast and their desire for recognition so great that they will endure any kind of hardship or humiliation just to become the center of attention, if only for a few days or moments.

This accounts for the idea many have that these individuals are engaged in self-punishment. This nonsense about self-punishment is so widely believed that it gives rise to the belief in sadism-masochism, which assumes that some people get pleasure from being hurt or from hurting others. To a degree this is true; they do inflict pain on each other. But the pain is *incidental.* The object of the game is to make one's self the center of attention and thus the favored child for at least a short time while the beating lasts. And then the making up that usually follows provides more goodies and sprinkles parsley on the dish!

Rebellion against outside authority—or shall we say, the illusion that there exists such a thing as outside authority—exists in a person only as long as he has not discovered his own inside authority! Until a person has *discovered and dares* to follow his own inner gleam, we may be sure of one thing: he will be leaning in either negative or positive dependence on someone outside himself! What else could he do if he has not developed self-reliance and not learned to stand independently? It is estimated that about 90% of the people live in positive dependence, in conformity!

The habit of rebellion, however, appears on such a wide basis and in so many forms everywhere that it is to be found also as a hidden part of positive conformity; like the dark side of the moon. Open revolt is relatively rare, whereas hidden revolt is pandemic. It includes pilfering, shoplifting, malingering, negligence, chronic lateness, sleeplessness, nervousness, psychosomatic ailments, nail biting, nose picking, disorderliness, and every other asocial or antisocial compulsion that exists. Everyone who does these things knows only too well that such activities are a way of secretly thumbing one's nose at parent figures and their surrogates.

Lacking self-reliance, we seek others and we are only too eager to obey them in order to escape facing our responsibilities and exercising our own initiative. It is so much easier to follow someone else and then blame him if things go wrong. But at the same time, we deeply resent our own *lack of initiative and bitterly envy those who have it.* We always hate those we lean upon or look up to. As Adler said, "No one likes to look up all the time since it makes the back of the neck tired." It is only to be expected, then, that we shall work up a load of envy-resentment against those we obey. Then we retaliate by some form of rebellion—some way of hitting back. If we can't hit back directly at the one we hate the most, we can hit back indirectly, by some hidden attack, such as shoplifting, nose-picking, taking drugs, alcohol or any other form of what appears to be self-sabotage.

The habit of rebellion and the accompanying, or implicit, self-sabotage is the revenge of a dependent individual against social demands which he cannot meet as an emotionally mature person. He tries, in effect, "to shame his parents when company is present" and thus to humiliate them, as he feels he has been humiliated and disciplined by them.

Much unhappiness will be avoided if parents, prison authorities, teachers and others who have executive or administrative jobs realize that *all forms of obedience* intend to induce subordination. An attitude of subordination or insubordination provokes the habit of rebellion as a reaction, which will be equal and opposite to the pressure of obedience. Positive obedience is fully as damaging to the individual as its idiot-twin, the habit of rebellion. And we must remember that we cannot have one without the other being present in *submerged form.* The delinquent is overtly rebellious but hides from himself his *innate dependent submissiveness*! And the openly submissive person betrays his rebellion by myriad forms of negativity, resistance, animosity, evasion, ineptness, clumsiness, apparent incompetence. He acts out the appearance of "I cannot" when it is evident to others that "he secretly wills not to participate in a useful way."

The habit of rebellion, then, is the price everyone must pay—through the nose—if he lacks his own authority, self-reliance! Rebellion is the evil smell of decayed self-reliance and is an inescapable symptom. The greatest mistake is to try to get rid of the habit of rebellion by bringing up heavier artillery, the firepower of authority, to try to break the will of the rebel. That only serves to develop his skill to resist pressures and drives him deeper into negativity. There is no way to break a human will! At least from the outside.

How is one to pull himself out of a habit of being negative? Especially when it has become a matter of prestige to hang on to one's contrary, disruptive behavior as if it were a badge of honor? The only hope for a rebel is to face the fact that he is a patsy. He is in the position of someone who habitually works—like Rip van Winkle—for others, but without being on their payroll and getting any profit for himself! He is working like Sisyphus—the Greek god condemned by Zeus to roll a stone to the top of a hill. It took him the whole day to roll it to the top, but when he let go of it at night, it rolled to the bottom of the hill again, and he was doomed to continue this for eternity.

When—and only when—the person realizes that his habit of rebellion is a curse that has not been laid upon him, but that he is *holding* on to as if it were a great treasure—*then he can let go of it.* The trap will open by itself. As long as the rebellious person fancies that he is giving a masterful performance and is the whole last act of Aida all by himself, he is getting subjective satisfactions from his dramatics. When he sees for the first time that he is more like a ham actor—playing to an empty house, with himself as his best and only audience, then he begins to stand on his own feet and see himself in his true perspective: as a leaning, dependent, juvenile, subaltern, negatively obedient person who has not yet found the self-reliance to act his present age.

# 9 / *Sex vs love*

There is no end to the number of real and pseudo-problems people can make out of their sexual preferences and relationships. In Western culture we have been led to believe that sex, love and marriage are a package job; if you manage to get one, the others will come along as a bonus. No wonder we are confused, since no area of human relations is so contaminated by myths and wishful thinking.

We are almost wholly irrational on the subject. The mention of sex seems to be the signal for everyone to lose his mind, rush out of his tent, mount his horse and ride off in all directions. Fear, superstition, guilt feelings, tradition and every degree of ignorance hold sway with hardly a challenge from our common sense. In fact, man's thinking about sex seems wholly devoid of common sense. Other animals make no such confusion about sex and do not fear it.

Hunger and sex are basic biological drives. Each is a kind, or variety, of hunger, and hunger of any kind is a tension that seeks release by fulfillment. What one likes to eat and the conditions under which he likes to eat it are highly personal choices. The same is equally true of the sexual appetite. This probably explains why both hunger and sex are so highly susceptible to being modified and conditioned by influences from the environment.

Tastes in food include almost everything that can be chewed and swallowed, including human flesh, if you happen to be a cannibal. The sexual urge can be satisfied in such a variety of ways that it is boring to catalogue them, as anyone knows it he has read Krafft-Ebing. The sex urge can adapt itself to any form of conditioning as easily as water can fit the shape of any vessel into which it is poured. The sex drive has no inherent goal of its own *except to achieve an orgasm.* But we must examine it with each individual to discover what other aspects of his personality it clings to and is reflecting in his behavior. Sex is always more than just sex; it picks up other demands, as a dog picks up ticks when it runs in the woods.

This point is very important to our understanding of

sexual behavior; it isn't just what it seems on the surface. Sex is not a field of causes; it is not the cause of the manner in which we express it: *sex is the field of results*! It is a mirror in which we reflect our own character accurately and fully. It is—what we are! We cannot be better or worse or different in the sexual area than we are in our over-all behavior. It does not follow a separate law that is contrary to, or apart from, our total personality. Each of us is predominantly either a giver or a taker in his approach to life. What we do about sex will follow the same basic pattern.

Sex is an automatic function, like swallowing or walking. It operates on an *on-off* basis, depending on the signals sent by our conditioned attitudes to the situation facing us. If this is understood, then we shall see that it operates when it is triggered, but the particular sexual preference is unique to each of us.

The erotic significance of a sexual act is not found in the act itself, and analysis will tell us nothing important about the actual preference. The erotic pattern depends on the degree of our self-reliance and will change only as we alter our whole approach to life. It cannot be changed as a thing apart. The dependent person will have a pattern of sexual demands shaped by the fact that he is a leaning, dependent person and demands much personal recognition. But if he becomes more self-sufficient emotionally and demands less pampering, his sexual demands, likes and dislikes will alter as he becomes liberated from his begging attitude. He will not demand so much of others but become a more active, giving person—a doer rather than a passive-receptive receiver of bounty from another.

From the above we see not much can be said about the sexual act itself or about sex as a biological drive isolated from its context, *the character of the individual.* But we find no end to the things we can say about how we use sex in our approach to others. It is easy to see how we twist it, cramp, expand, distort and modify it. And how it manages somehow to curl itself around anything presented to it, much as a vine can find a way to climb up the face of a wall if necessary. It gets where it wants to go: an orgasm. And it manages to do so regardless of whether it uses traditional or disapproved paths to its end.

Sex and love are not the same thing at all. They can coexist, although they are quite often found apart. We have not been trained to recognize love and hardly know what to look for, especially if it is not the same as sex. The ancient Greeks had no such problem. They recognized two kinds of love and had two separate words for them: agape and eros. We have only the word love to express both of them, although in expression they are worlds apart *and never the twain shall meet.* As a matter of fact, agape and eros are mutually exclusive; when eros comes in, agape goes out, just as the bird flies away when the cat comes by.

Eros is nothing more than infantile possessiveness. When someone says he loves ice cream, you have no doubt what he plans to do with it. Eros refers to likes, preferences, desires and all aspects of acquisitiveness. It always implies *partiality*. We prefer the part and reject what remains outside our preference. Eros is a stick that has two ends: attraction and aversion, love and hate, for and against, toward and away—from things or people. It implies a critical, evaluative, judgmental, separative, hidden, fault-finding attitude toward the world and others. We are enslaved by the things we love—and equally by those we hate. Our desire to possess becomes a rope that ties us to the object of our desire; it then *controls us* in our effort to hold on to it. Eros restricts our initiative and limits it to the exact degree that we wish to own and control the object of our love. Our likes and dislikes, our loves, become a prison of our own construction, and the penalty we must pay for any partiality we may show for one thing or person above another. We cannot free ourselves while we hold on to preferences and make them the monitor of our behavior.

Agape is a wholly different kind of love. It is entirely nonpossessive and demands nothing for itself. It does not judge, discriminate, evaluate. It is wholly nonpartisan and is regarded as the attitude and nature of God, who "sends rain on the just and the unjust alike." Impartially, non-judgmentally, uncritically! Perhaps the words of Lao-Tzu—as interpreted by Archie Bahm—can give us some inkling of what such love is like:

*The intelligent man is not wishful.*
*He accepts what others wish for themselves as his wish for them.*

*Those who appear as good, he accepts,*
*And those who appear as bad, he accepts;*
*For Nature accepts both.*

*Those who appear faithful, he accepts,*
*And those who appear unfaithful, he accepts;*
*For Nature accepts both.*

*The intelligent man treats every kind of nature impartially,*
*And wishes good to one as much as another.*

This kind of impersonal interest certainly has no resemblance to the usual, feverish, anxiety-ridden attachment we commonly think of as being in love. It is a desire to see things grow according to their own natural bent, so that they express their full inner potential without being limited by our demands on them. Agape is free of any desire to have love returned and does not depend on any recognition for itself. As they say: old men plant trees!

They obviously do not expect to sit under their shade or eat fruit of them, but they plant trees out of fullness and gratitude and the joy they experience in the life they are living themselves.

Impersonal love is the only kind that does not have a curse inherent in it. All forms of possessiveness or attachment have their own built-in punishment. Desire cannot be separated from pain and disappointment. Oscar Wilde said that the only thing worse than not getting what we want is getting it. Desire is born out of dependence and the feeling of emptiness it produces. It breeds greed, because the feeling of emptiness *cannot be compensated.* Impersonal love, on the other hand, arises out of a feeling of self-sufficiency, fullness, capacity, confidence and strength, instead of a feeling of need and poverty. It has no reason to seek anything outside itself. It does not make a hell of its own in which to destroy itself. We destroy the thing we love under eros; we consume and are consumed in the relationship.

The leaning, dependent individual, however, finds it difficult to imagine any love other than eros. The person who habitually seeks close attachments, with all their bickerings, mutual controls, hurt feelings, misunderstandings, boredom, banality, cannot imagine how he would get any satisfaction or warmth in a nonpossessive relationship. He is so accustomed to the tensions, anxieties, hostilities, uncertainties of the struggle to possess, dominate and use the partner, that impersonal enjoyment of some thing or person appears flat and flavorless to him. Even though he complains bitterly about the unhappiness of eros, he is most reluctant to give it up. He wants only the good end of the stick but without the bad end coming along with it.

How do we recognize agape at work around us? Adler called it "social interest." It is everywhere, but we are usually oblivious to it because it is obvious. The moment we begin to look, we become aware of it in almost every area. Love makes the world go round, is the old saying. Surely we cannot imagine that it is that contentious, possessive, quarrelsome, larcenous, murderous eros that makes the world go round. Nothing divides and cripples individuals, communities, groups more than the grasping, ambitious efforts of eros. Both its positive and negative aspects—love and hate—are the obvious source of endless friction and unhappiness. We cannot believe this is what makes the world do anything but commit violence!

We know intuitively and at once that it is agape that holds the world together and agape that keeps the race alive, certainly not the competitive jealousy of eros! Agape not only causes old men to plant trees, it is at the root of the greatest outpouring of impersonal, constructive interest known to man: Thorstein Veblen's "*the spirit of workmanship*." Agape is the child making sand castles at the beach. He is wholly lost in the process of what he is doing. He has no trace of self-consciousness and not a shred of need for recognition or outside help of any kind. He is both the doer and the deed! He is the Creator and the creation. His action is its own reward; it is a light that casts no shadow. *Agape is love that has no object!* It dances just to dance and sings just to sing. It has no aim and no motive!

When we open our eyes to the spirit of workmanship, we suddently see it on every side. The bus driver pulls out of the puddle on a rainy day so that we do not have to step into it when we get off. He didn't have to do that for us; it was agape that did it for us. Some of them do and some of them don't. Then there is the trader who conscientiously seeks to improve the quality of his merchandise without charging a robber-baron price for it. As Lao-Tzu says: "The generous trader needs no scales." And there is the physician, exhausted after a day of work and loss of sleep, who keeps up with developments in his field to be able to pass them on to his patients who depend on him. There are untold numbers of such unsung heros who investigate, explore, experiment, and otherwise go out of their way with no thought of ultimate reward except for the joy of the journey itself. The process is its own reward, and it is that which keeps them happy. They feel no hardship, no effort, no resistance.

The spirit of workmanship is the inner gleam at work. It is the boy playing with his blocks; it is the creator evolving new forms on the Grazing Principle as he lives intimately with life in the here-and-now. Such is agape and it is not puffed up. As St. Paul reminds us in his statement on the nature of agape:

> Though I speak with the tongues of men and of angels, and have not charity [love], I am become as sounding brass, or a tinkling cymbal. And though I give my body to be burned, and have not charity, it profiteth me nothing. Charity suffereth long, and is kind; charity envieth not; charity vaunteth not itself, is not puffed up, doth not behave itself unseemly, seeketh not her own, is not easily provoked, thinketh no evil; rejoiceth not in iniquity, but rejoiceth in the truth; beareth all things, believeth all things, hopeth all things, endureth all things. Charity never faileth. . . .

In other words, it is the agape and not the competitive envy that makes life both enduring and endurable for us. No amount of success can make up to an individual for his own lack of agape. Above all, agape is nonjudgmental; we do not condemn ourself or others.

Let us face the fact: how else can we endure life on this earth unless we can achieve a large degree of tolerance of oneself and others? Life is far too painful if we are hypersensitive and look for the flaws in everything. Nor can we endure life if we are coldly indifferent and insensitive to others. Not being attached means we are not clinging to, or demanding of, others; it certainly does not mean that we are aloof and wooden. We remain vital and in contact with ourselves and others only when we accept our own nature, without any wishful thinking, and accept others on exactly the same non-judgmental basis. Only then can we hope to achieve the intimacy, spontaneity and awareness with our own true nature and those around us.

It is easy to see how different sexual behavior will be under eros and under agape. Eros is the defective love life of the leaning, dependent person, simply because he is incapable of anything more than *seeking and taking* in his relationships; he is not yet *a giver or a doer.* Eros is still the child in us that remains at the original nutritional level, using every device—political and physical—to exploit, dominate and possess the object.

The dependent person loves anyone who will pamper him and is interested in using eros to replace the emotional and physical support given us originally by our parents. He is incapable of agape and must fall back on manipulation or violence to enslave the partner on whom he leans. He loves the person while he is being pampered but turns to violence the moment the pampering is denied him. Thus the dependent person hates the one he loves. A man killed his sweetheart. When asked why he did it, he said that she wanted to leave him, but that he loved her so much he couldn't stand the thought of someone else getting her. Such crimes of passion and rape are easily understood as expressions of eros. And eros is obviously behind sadistic-masochistic attachments, as well as similar mutually exploitive sexual relationships.

Eros is prone to all forms of pathological distortions, and it easily forms possessive-dependent relationships on any level. Some seek sex with children, as described in the novel *Lolita,* since they belive children are more easily dominated and used. Or they seek relationships with members of minority groups, in the hope that it will be easier to maintain an easy position of dominance over them. Some who dare not approach others have sexual relations with an object which they steal from the person they overvalue. The lack of emotional self-reliance always finds some way to use the one it leans on. If we feel we cannot stand alone, we always seek some false security in trying to make someone else our contact person. We expect them to love us and be our seeing-eye dog who leads us to salvation.

People resist our efforts to use them, so it is easy to see why relationships based on eros can never be free of struggles for dominance and endless manipulation of each other. Eric Berne details many of these efforts in his book called *Games People Play.* Such games are numberless, but at bottom, it is always the familiar old game of one-upmanship. Only the relations based on agape can be kind and nonexploitive, since those individuals do not need to profit at the expense of the loved one. They do not need to be loved back to avoid emotional bankruptcy.

We must examine the area of friendships in the light of eros and agape. Since most of us are leaning conformists, we must expect that most of the friendships in the world will be based on fear and a competitive desire to use each other for personal advantage. Agape, however, is impartially friendly and plays no favorites. It has no need for partisanship and therefore is not to be found among those people huddled in fear like puppies in a basket trying to keep warm. Agape love is not for hire!

We have explained that agape is the lifeblood of the community. If we had only the easily destroyed friendships of eros, the force that holds society together would soon fall below a critical level and that would be the end of us. We would destroy ourselves out of our own boundless greed! It obviously takes more than old men to plant trees! A predatory society without agape is unthinkable and could never survive. There are many varieties of limited friendships that can exist in which the exploitation and greed are held down by a principle of "you scratch my back, I'll scratch yours." These are pay-as-you-go friendships and keep us on our toes. They are not agape friendships, but they force us to give as good as we expect to get. That obligates us to put something in the pot and not sit on our haunches like kennel dogs and howl complaints if we do not get everything for nothing. At least, we can't approach others empty-handed and expect to deal with them.

One of the most common forms of limited association, or eros friends, grows out of having the same prejudices, likes and dislikes, social background, snob values with each other—clans, political parties, religious groups and similar organizations that exist to promote their own welfare. The more insecure and dependent the individuals, the stronger the tie that binds them.

Such groups either provide or pay for a shaky feeling of security from associating with each other for protection, as it says in the old prayerbook, "against things that go bump in the night." For their own survival these groups try to reduce the interpersonal rivalries, hostility and competition among members so that they are less damaging to each other than would otherwise be the case. As long as the members conform to the mores of the group and no one tries to lord it over the others too openly, they limp along in a kind of togetherness as best they can at their present stage of defective self-reliance.

To the extent people feel weak and unable to stand alone, they are attracted to such organizations as something to lean on for the strength they do not have. This explains the success of Hitler's youth groups and his whole movement that grew out of the competitive envy of the people of that time. This pseudo-fraternal solidarity hides the fears and dependence from their eyes and also from each other, so that they appear successful to each other and to themselves.

One of the more pathetic or amusing levels of eros friendship amounts to mutual baby-sitting of one adult by another. Those who remember the film *Marty* can recall how the gang assembled on the corner nightly trying to find something to do to occupy their time. Not one of them was able to entertain himself, and each was leaning on the other to think of something for them to do to keep from going stir-crazy.

The usual bridge or garden club and other quasi-study groups are similar examples of such activity. The individuals lack the ability to program and structure their own leisure time and fall back on some social gang to do it for them, to escape their own personal responsibility and initiative. Each agrees to act as the baby-sitter of the others. They invent busyness to hide their irresponsibility and the emptiness of their own emotional lives. The ostensible purpose of the group is to do good in the community. But each knows the little secret; none is able to think of anything more personal to do than this pretense of good will, which they use to hide the fact that they all belong to the army of the emotionally unemployed! Their competitive envy finds its expression in the usual backbiting and club politics that is par for the course.

Perhaps the most damaging, pernicious form of eros masquerades as a close loving family. The kind which—as the slogan goes—stays together! The whole function of the family should be *to prepare the child to stand alone after puberty* and go his own independent way to do whatever he has in him to do. The aim of a family is certainly *not to stay together*! Each of us must become a full individual in his own right and not limit or hobble others. But eros is endlessly possessive.

Parents with this mistaken concept cripple their children and make them fearful of finding their own way confidently in life. Agape releases us to go directly onto the Grazing Principle, so that we can follow our own inner gleam in maturity. Close family ties deny growth and freedom to the members of such blighted families, and they watch each other jealously lest one escape the hold the others have on him. Members do not dare move separately or apart without hurting poor mama's feelings —or each other's feelings, which is even a worse state of affairs.

No one has the right to live vicariously through another. The parents and siblings of such incestuous families destroy each other, because such relationships deny freedom of the spirit. Agape liberates; eros enslaves. There is no middle ground of partial slavery. Those who want to end free or live free must start free! Wishful thinking cannot change this fact.

# 10 / *Marriage for the millions*

There is no relationship in the world that is a more rugged test of self-reliance than marriage. Here again, we find that what happens in the relationship depends on whether the marriage partners are trying to meet on the level of agape or on the infantile, possessive level of eros.

As we all know, most marriages are struggling along on unmitigated, unadulterated eros. A tiger in every tank! Such marriages, built on possessiveness, have a system of inescapable punishments. The institution cannot stand the strain of a dominance-submission struggle. The adults are damaged, and any children of the union are damaged from the glancing psychological blows aimed by the parents at each other.

The majority of marriages are made unhappy by the myth of romance. But there is another factor that presents endless trouble: the fear and distrust between the sexes. Now we can show how it is used for warfare in marriage. The fear that exists between the sexes gives rise to a struggle for dominance as to which one will have rule over the other. This gives rise to the leader-follower, or master-slave, relationship. The independence of both individuals is lost in this struggle wherein one tries to sit on the other. Their fears of each other are increased as each wins bloody victories over the other. It is commonly described as a battle to see "which will wear the pants." Freud went way out on a limb and described it as the female envy of the male penis. A lot she cares about that. Frightened people want power. But *what they need* is more self-reliance and productivity.

Marriages based on the romantic myth break down into mutual blame. The purpose of blame is to hide from oneself the necessity to become more self-reliant and productive. Blame says, "You are a dog for not giving me what I want of you." It does not urge us to get over our own leaning, dependent attitude. We would not feel let down if we had not been leaning on someone. Blame is only a way of putting the whole job on the other fellow.

Dr. Alfred Adler used to say that marriage should be a partnership of two people for the world and not a side show of two people against the world. Or against each other. There is no room for mutual exploitation. Adler, told that Miss X was going to be married, commented, "Against whom?" Adler knew Miss X well. We can guess the probable success of any marriage if we know the degree of self-reliance of the contracting parties. The success of a marriage cannot be greater than the productivity of the partners.

Most marriages in our civilization begin with the illusion of romantic love. The best definition of romance is: the desire to be pampered. Pampering is the desire for personal recognition. In short, it is evidence of persistent infantilism and a lack of self-reliance. It is the desire to "expect from another." It is the opposite of the creative attitude, which "gives out" rather than "sucks in." In romantic love, each one expects to "get" happiness from the other. The partner is supposed to pamper him. Both sit and wait for the other one to get busy. A row begins when the show doesn't start on time.

The infantile attitude toward marriage is almost unbelievable. We can only guess at the extent of it when we realize the number of love stories that are ground out and consumed each month for books, periodicals, TV, radio, movies and the like. People would not buy such stuff if they did not believe in its probability. We find no such sale for fairy stories, which are no more fantastic. After stuffing ourselves with such material, is it any wonder that partners resent each other when they find out that marriage is mostly "When do we eat?" and related mundane questions?

Brought up on the infantile pabulum of romance, a young couple is led to imagine that marriage is a box full of goodies that any couple can buy at the license bureau. They are "reliably" informed that they can sit down and eat out of this box all their lives and it will never be empty. Marriage is a box, and it can be bought for a few dollars. But it is empty. There will never be anything in it unless the partners put it there! And if they do not want it to be empty, they must put in a lot more than they are in the habit of taking out. But the young romantic who imagined it ought to be endlessly full of goodies institutes a lawsuit against God and the marriage partner as soon as he discovers the score of the game. He feels swindled. But he imagines the next box he buys will be full even though the first one was empty.

Marriage was never intended to do anything for people! Certainly it was not designed to make them happy. People are supposed to do something for marriage. And who wants such a raw deal as that in this age of easy profits? It is advertised as a get-rich-quick scheme. But it is only a gimmick of society for the protection and education of children. It requires the combined work of male and female to make a successful, productive unit in society.

Marriage has little or no relationship to happiness. Happiness is a by-product of a self-reliant, productive, creative way of life. The individual who has not learned to be happy single has just as little chance being happy in marriage. It can never be an escape from responsibility into which infantile adults can flee from self-development. Those who have the begging attitude will find the pickings poor in marriage. Beggars never get rich or happy. The marriage partner is not to be recruited as a baby-sitter for an infantile adult. At least, not for long.

Surely the most destructive factors that prevent adjustment in marriage are part of the sin of obedience. Examination will show that many evils we hear about stem from the same source. Comedians have practically earned their livings with jokes about in-laws. Mothers-in-law are always pictured as interfering in their children's marriages. Or the children are still under the domination of their parents in spite of being married and having children of their own. The fact that it is so widespread as to be considered a joke only indicates the amount of infantile obedience that persists in the average adult.

This lack of self-reliance on the part of such adults is justified by the obedient notion that they must "show respect." This dependent, obedient attitude has nothing to do with respect. It is only the begging attitude of "Please don't hit me." Respect for others, including our parents, means to regard them as equal adults who have a right to their own life just as we have a right to ours.

Each must learn to please himself—first on a self-reliant basis.

In the story of the creation of man in the Old Testament, this concept of self-reliance is made very clear: "Therefore shall a man leave his father and his mother, and shall cleave unto his wife; and they shall be one flesh." In short, the only right attitude toward in-laws that do not mind their own business is summed up in the slogan: "Throw the rascals out."

Marriage is here to stay. Right or wrong, hot or cold, people will continue to get married. Even the most primitive civilizations have the institution. No social or political order will ever be invented without it. We had better understand it. Marriage is the gimmick used in each society so that the local witch doctor, medicine man, milkman, diaper service and others know where to send the bill for their work. If the human infant developed as rapidly as other animal babies, our society and its institutions would be vastly different. As things stand, the world is organized mainly to guarantee the survival of the next generation. Adults come off only second best, as is reasonable to expect.

The baby turtle is in business for himself from the moment he is hatched. He never sees his parents and couldn't care less. Most other baby animals are able to shift for themselves as adults within two or three years. But the human animal requires about fifteen years before it is of much use to itself or anyone else. For this reason, mainly, the human animal will always find it necessary to live in a group. For the purpose of mutual assistance for survival, the human infant is a total loss as far as being any help. He must be supported, educated, protected for about a fourth of his whole life span. Someone has to be charged with this responsibility.

In most places in the world, this is understood quite well. In most older cultures, a young couple of marriage age are aware of what will be expected of each of them. They know that the tribe, or group, expects them to be a team. *He* will have the job of doing certain things, and *she* will have different duties. It is understood that they are about to enter a *working relationship* and to remain productive! Neither the male nor the female goes into marriage empty-handed. Neither expects to be taken care of at the expense of the other one or at the expense of the social group. The parents of the children usually arrange the marriage, carefully weighing the preparation of the prospective partners' ability to carry out the job.

Most of them never heard of romance. And they would certainly not regard it as any basis for getting married. The real problems of marriage are not whether John loves Mary and Mary loves John. The real problems will always be "When do we eat?" "What do we eat?" "Where do we eat?" "How much do we eat?" "Where do we go when it rains or snows?" "What do we wear?" "Can we produce enough to feed the children?" "Can we train them to grow up to be a help and not remain a burden?"

There can be no happiness for us unless we are able to accomplish the basic demands. Any tendency to overlook or disregard these tasks only leads to trouble for all concerned. People entering marriage should be prepared to face and answer these questions as the *main concern* of marriage. Society does not give a fig whether marriage partners find happiness together as long as they pay their bills and do their job. And any realistic marriage should begin with this in mind. Whatever happiness the pair may create must somehow fit within the general limits of this picture. They have no chance unless they begin with the facts.

Before leaving the subject of marriage, we ought to look at what often passes as marriage counseling. Much, if not most, of it is an effort to hide the facts. In place of the realities which sound so unattractive to those who want to be pampered, counseling often devotes itself to placating the injured parties. "Ten Tiny Techniques for Titillating the Marriage Partner" are often suggested. These are only ways of maintaining the slavery of ancient Egypt instead of making the partners free, productive, creative members of a team. Marriage is still kept in the category of a stranglehold, and nothing is done to ventilate the sweat box of romantic nonsense.

There is far too much concern with keeping the marriage intact. Advice is given to each as to how to pamper the other one. Endless articles are published in slick magazines for women as to "How to Hold Your Husband." How unfair of anyone to try to hold another! Our whole effort must be to try to pry open the clenched fist each one has on the other. Their hands should be free for productivity. They should not be engaged in mutual "snooper-vision" and in trying to hold each other.

All human relationships must be open on all sides for growth. We must hold each other in an open palm. If we give honest weight and full measure, we need have no anxiety. The partner cannot get a better deal elsewhere. If he wanders, he will soon return. The shop that gives the most for the price gets the business most of the time. Free, productive partners tend to grow apace rather than to grow apart! And no law will hold people together unless they are at about the same level of development. We get the kind of partner we deserve, according to our own degree of infantilism. One partner may like to imagine he is superior to the other. But if this were so, why is he hanging around so long? Just out of the goodness of his heart? Well, hardly! Or only for the sake of the children? That is a laugh, too. He or she hangs on for the same reason a cripple hangs on to his crutch. He does not yet know how to walk on his own feet unassisted. He wants to continue on the infantile crutches of praise and blame rather than increase his own self-reliance and productivity. The main job in marriage counseling is to stop the blame and dependence in favor of getting each partner back into production once again. Or for the first time, if that should be the case.

Marriage, as we have said, is here to stay. Properly undertaken, it can be a fruitful relationship in which both partners can grow stronger in their own potentialities and not of necessity become a rubber stamp. On a mistaken basis, it is a hair shirt, a sweat box, a stranglehold and an endless punishment for our infantilism. The begging attitude keeps us beggars. Obedience keeps us slaves. Creativeness, alone, can free us.

# 11 / *The manipulators*

The habit of manipulating other people as a means of achieving our personal welfare is learned in childhood; it is the only way the child has in the beginning for getting what he seeks for his development. It is not a wrong action at that time of life. But it is the root of all behavioral evils if we continue this habit *after adolescence*. It is the root of all neurosis, crime and other similar destructive activity. Nothing is more important for us as individuals than to be fully aware of those areas in which we are still depending on others. *Depending on others makes manipulation inevitable.* If we can, we must exploit. This is like standing on tiptoe, and as Lao-Tzu says, the man who stands on tiptoe must keep running.

Man is a manipulator of his environment. He has in his power the ability to remake the surface of the earth, to free himself of diseases, poverty, war, crime and similar worldwide evils. But this is only possible if he manages to educate himself for total self-reliance. We must be taught to *manipulate circumstance* in the impersonal outside world and to give up the childish habit of *manipulating each other,* as is now the common habit. Most of us depend on those around us, on dead tradition and custom for our direction, instead of thinking and acting on our own; this makes us conformists. We do not act, we merely react to what others do.

Whether a child or a dependent adult, we are obliged to develop and employ the political arts of manipulating others simply because we have no choice; we cannot function independently. Our lack of self-reliance gives us no alternative other than to fall back on the habits of our childhood and use those old tricks as a way of pressuring others into doing what we want of them. The crybaby cries; the impatient one has temper tantrums; the inactive one sulks and acts melancholy. These are but a few ways we use to disturb others and to make them serve our wishes.

Those who lack self-reliance have no alternative but to live or die by their ability to exploit others. It is not just a figure of speech to say that a person is driven into a life of crime or neurosis. If we have not developed physical and emotional self-sufficiency and must therefore depend on our ability to supply our needs through others by influencing them to serve us, we often run out of ways to bring pressures on them. At that point, we are driven to attack them more openly to get our way.

When the mature individual faces a need, he puts his mind to the circumstances surrounding the problem and invents a way to manipulate the elements that need to be changed. He is a doer of deeds and finds no reason to push others around or otherwise exert personal exploitative dominance over them. And by the same token, he does not need to fight to be the center of attention or to seek personal recognition as an individual. His self-confidence is based on his ability to achieve his goals and is in no way held up by, or dependent on, the opinion of others.

The dependent individual must use others *as his crutches* and he cannot go either *farther* or *faster* than he can influence his crutches to carry him. And he suffers the habitual frustration of someone who must use crutches; he loves them since he can't move without them and he hates them bitterly for the same reason. But the dependent person can never hope to know the enduring happiness of self-sufficiency. That wonderful feeling is reserved only for those who *stand alone* emotionally without leaning on others outside themselves. There is no such thing as good attachment; good slavery does not exist.

The source of all our emotional pain lies in this persisting infantilism, which is only a refusal on the part of the individual to give up his childhood habits and grow up. A child is unavoidably a *consumer of goods and services* provided him by others. Little or nothing is expected of him in return. An adult, however, is expected to become a producer of goods and services and to give his product in exchange for those of others. The child is passive-receptive. But, at some stage of the game, he has to give up his *getting* style-of-life and become an active-productive member of his community.

I. A. R. Wylie said, "Many people go from infancy to senility without ever achieving maturity." In short, many retain the grasping, acquisitive, possessive qualities of the child throughout life and resist any pressure of the environment to make them spend either themselves or their goods for what they demand. It is the nature of an infant to pick up anything it can get and put it in its mouth indiscriminately, whether it is food or carpet tacks. And since habit never rests, we never fully get over our grasping, possessive habits. Our only hope of being relieved of them is to be wholly *aware of what* they are doing at all times. We must know the face of our enemy under any mask it may be wearing at the moment.

We must regard ourselves as having three main levels

of development, or age levels. Our chronological age grows by itself, a year at a time, and no one has found a way to retard that in any way. Our mental age, or intelligence quotient, varies with the individual. But, even so, most of the population is normal or above; there are relatively few really mentally defective individuals. It is the third factor that causes all the trouble. That is *the self-reliance factor, on which all others must depend for their fulfillment.* Regardless of age and intellect, we cannot hope to meet the conditions of the outside world if we are defective in this area. All of our emotional crippling arises from a stunted or retarded growth of self-reliance.

Self-reliance is a factor that has to be developed; it does not grow by itself as the body does. Each of us is born weak and completely helpless. We have no choice but to lean and depend on the adults who take care of us. Our formative years are spent in the role of second-class citizen who must accept the will of others because he cannot stand on his own feet yet. No one of us escapes this dependent role as his beginning. And, as habit never rests, it is not surprising that many—if not most—of us continue through life to put other heads higher than our own and then try to lean and depend on such pseudo-authority figures, as if they had all the answers to our welfare and contentment, exactly as in that period when we were children.

When a child is confronted by a problem, he turns to

someone else for the solution. He seeks someone whom he can enslave or influence to serve his purposes. Each of us has passed through this helpless-child phase, and it is no mystery why all of us have a large measure of larceny in our hearts.

As soon as the child discovers his helplessness and his need to manipulate people to influence them to serve him, he begins to develop the skills of the politician. He throws himself into the influence game and soon discovers there are two ways of exploiting others. His smiles ingratiate and flatter people into serving him. Most people are easily trapped by flattery, and thus he is able to get them to go into the outside world and bring back the prizes he wants for himself. But if this political strategy fails him, he learns that he can intimidate adults by giving them a hotfoot, that is, by making them uncomfortable until they do his bidding. In other words, our earliest contacts with people imprint upon our budding nervous system a sly knowledge and subtle experience of exploitation pointing toward a master-slave, or dominance-submission, pattern in later life.

It is plain to see how this emotionally immature adult is really a person with "servant problems." He is constantly confronted by the task of finding ways to *get others to serve him and grant him special privileges and special exemptions.* His tragedy lies in the fact that he cannot *go directly on target* when facing a problem, since he has not trained himself to approach the world independently. His life is limited to those few things he is able to manipulate people into doing for him. He can only *look with envy* on others who are able to *serve themselves* and not have to stand in line as second-class citizens on the dole.

It is apparent then why it is useless to send a boy to do a man's job. The problems of the outside world demand initiative and spontaneity; a man must—like a swordsman—improvise his activity and defenses, depending on the thrusts of his enemy. He cannot wait for outside help or even think of it, and no dependency can help him in any way. He must be free in mind and body. He has no time to think.

Many people who earn their own living and pay their way financially imagine they are wholly independent. It is, of course, important for everyone to pay his own way financially, but we must remember that self-reliance exists at two levels. We have to stand secure at the physical *and the emotional* level. Both levels are equally important. Either alone is not enough.

# 12 / *Emotional self-reliance*

Many individuals learn how to take care of themselves physically, earn a living, build a business or profession, manage a family and otherwise conduct themselves with much success in public and private affairs. Yet they may fail in their human relationships, become alcoholic, tyrannical, depressed, psychotic, neurotic and be an emotional burden on all those around them—simply because they have not learned emotional self-reliance.

The indications of emotional dependence are easily evident at all stages of our lives. We cannot hide them from anyone but ourselves, for they are obvious in almost everything we do. We are what we do! And what we do is the real answer to what we mean and intend. What we say is neither here nor there, unless it is in agreement with our actions.

If we have trained ourselves to be alert to indications of emotional dependence, we quickly see them in what we do as well as what others around us are doing. If we are not alert to such indications, we may be *defeated by the most obvious habits of our daily life.* We may be oblivious to the obvious, our grasping dependency. We want to be loved and accepted by everyone and we can be deeply hurt if they resist, or are indifferent to, our expectation.

It is estimated that only about 10 percent of the population has developed emotional self-reliance. Every employer and school teacher is aware that most of the people they direct learn to do fairly well so long as someone keeps an eye on them and *acts as a kindly pacemaker parent* on whom they can lean for advice. When they are told what to do and taught how to do it, they follow along reasonably well until something happens that demands *personal initiative.* At this point, they dissolve into feelings of insecurity and fall apart until someone rescues them from their dilemma. They have never solved the problem of emotional self-reliance and do not know how to *stand alone*!

Each year that passes, more and more children are being sent to school before they have even a *minimum degree of emotional or physical self-reliance.* It has become a habit in our culture to do more and more for children and to expect less and less of them. Even the toothpaste commercial mother is now considered normal when she gives up expecting a child to brush his teeth without her *riding on his back.* Physical weaning is certainly more than teaching a child to give up the breast for solid food! It should include the idea that he learn to "be a help and not a burden" to those around him. He should *have been weaned of demanding special help and special consideration from his family,* so that when he goes to school he will not feel shocked at the impersonal atmosphere he meets with. If he has been overprotected at home, he expects personal help and attention from others outside the family. He wants most of his demands and needs granted without any effort on his part. And if he is let down, he *lacks the self-reliance to do things for himself,* so that he immediately begins to *fall behind those* who are more self-reliant and adequate to life's demands.

More and more children are being labeled mentally retarded as they fall behind in school. They are not necessarily mentally retarded. It is useless to expect that a child lacking in physical self-reliance will be able to meet the demands of school work that requires him to work independently. No teacher or mother can *do our learning for us.* They can hold up our pants for us in other ways, but intellectual development demands that the child show some willingness to pay attention and make an effort for himself. The more a child is deprived of his physical, and especially of his emotional, self-sufficiency, the greater the chance of his failing from the beginning of his school career.

The ability to *think* and *act* independently is an inherent capacity. There is no excuse for it being defective in about 90 percent of us; it is something everyone needs and everyone can have if he will train himself. No one is born with self-reliance, but nothing can stop us from achieving it if that is what we want. It begins when we are determined to do everything we can possibly do for ourselves, emotionally and physically, in preference to seeking someone to do it for us. Thus we get rid of our craving for special privilege and special exemptions. With this attitude, our physical self-sufficiency grows rapidly.

Our basic temperament is directly related to this factor of physical and emotional self-reliance. Someone has said that the world is made up of two kinds of people—those who love and those who hate. This isn't far from wrong. The fortunate 10 percent who are prepared to meet life on an independent basis show it in everything they do. They seem to pour themselves out on things as if they were pouring water on parched earth. They seem to have limitless resources and no fear of running dry. They live as if they feel that the world is a good place to be, and they do not feel disturbed if they find things less than perfect. When blocked in one direction, they merely take another and have fun either way.

The person lacking in self-reliance, physically and emotionally, has to count his pennies all the way. Nothing comes easy to him, and he complains bitterly about almost everything. He resists the demands of life and is envious of those around him. His main effort is to evade demands and to withhold himself as much as possible. He blames everyone and everything and is always seeking causes of his defeats. He is the spoil-sport and the Monday-morning quarterback. What he gains is no joy to him because he feels that it is so much less than what is due him. He is a grudge collector and usually has a lawsuit against God waiting in the courts.

It is evident that the self-reliant person habitually minimizes the dangers ahead of him, whereas the one lacking in self-sufficiency habitually exaggerates them. This factor of individual temperament is most important to an individual, as it sets all the *over-all climate* in which he plays out his whole life. The self-reliant person regards life as an interesting game that is fun to play, and he feels that life has very few irremediable mistakes and difficulties. But the emotionally dependent person lives as if he were the major figure in a Greek tragedy; or, as someone has said, "like an accident going somewhere to happen." He acts as if threatened on all sides.

Self-reliance, then, is the greatest gift any parent can give a child, for it is a habit of mind that follows him all his life and levels the mountains before him as he goes. No less fortunate, however, is the person who later in life has discovered that his difficulties arise from a lack of self-reliance. His awareness of this basic fact releases the trap in which he has found himself, and he gives up his juvenile dependence!

# 13 / *Trust only movement*

Alfred Adler built the approach to his theory of Individual Psychology on the admonition: "Trust only movement." See what happens—not what you feel should or ought to happen in a situation. He was deeply aware that life happens at the level of events, not of words, and is always outside our ability to grasp it intellectually.

No book can ever adequately encompass the truth by piling up facts and information. Every writer is faced with a hopeless task and may confuse the reader by encouraging dependency on a how-to-do-it basis. It is impossible to trap life between the covers of a book, just as it is impossible to get a bagful of wind or a bucketful of river.

Any effort to do this will end up with a bag of dead air or a bucket of stagnating water.

Life is a movement! As one writer said, "Life is the thing that really happens to us while we are making other plans." The mystery we call life cannot be trapped by words. The best that any concept, word, idea or language can do for readers is to "point outside and beyond themselves" to the living now of what is, which is so vast that one cannot even imagine it. The tragedy of the person with a dependent mind is that he does not look at where the finger points; instead, he clings desperately to the finger and tries to suck nourishment from it.

Oriental philosophies are much more aware of the vastness of reality and the incapacity of the human mind to grasp it in verbal concepts. Much of their imagery is built around an attempt to portray the incomprehensibility of the *whole* in which we move, such as the description of Indra's net. Indra's net, we are told, extends in all directions—to infinity. Each knot in the net is a golden bead. On each bead is the reflection of all the other beads! And on each reflection is the reflection of the reflections of all other beads.

Indra's net suggests the complete relatedness and inseparability of everything in the whole universe. But, at the same time, it suggests the complete separateness and individuality of every person and thing. All objects partake of being both one and many! Separate and not separate! Every end is a beginning and every beginning an end. Life is both unknowable and unspeakable—whereby language can become a trap for dependent minds.

A classic example of confusion that exists at word level is the familiar seven deadly sins. These sins are solemnly listed as envy, pride, anger, greed, lust, sloth and gluttony; they are guaranteed to do you in! In fact, they will—but for a very simple reason. All seven of them turn out to be, on observation, nothing more than a *clinical* listing of symptoms! These symptoms are *inseparable* from the infantile, leaning, dependent habit of mind.

What a letdown! The seven deadly sins turn out to be nothing more than little toadstools that have sprung up around the dead roots of a decayed self-reliance. These highly touted sins are only names we give to petty forms of exploitation that we turn to if we have not learned to stand on our own two feet.

The person who has achieved self-reliance has no need for the piddling gains he can get by exploiting the so-called deadly sins. He finds neither gain nor pleasure in their pursuit. His self-reliance has safely removed him from the needs of dependency. He can create his own vitality and *does not need to steal or beg it.* The so-called sinner is nothing more than an unhappy child with messy pants!

When we speak of someone being a failure as a human

being, we know that he is incapable of acting the role of an emotionally self-reliant adult. We know this regardless of how much money he has made or what prestige he has gained in a particular area of skill. Failure implies failure to function as an adult—someone lacking in self-sufficiency! At the core of such inadequate behavior, we always see the infant seeking personal recognition from those around him. He is marked by this begging attitude or by his arrogant demands.

A mature adult finds no need to beg. He is an explorer and a doer. He does not have to compete and aspire to be the favored one. Only the child or the infantile adult has to worry about *his status in the eyes of* those around him.

It is a matter of much interest in the Old Testament that the third story is one of sibling rivalry in which each brother wanted to be the favored child. (The second story is about the fall of man when he aspired to "be as a God.") It will always be thus with children, for this is the nature of the child. Every child wants to be the only child. And it is possible that this urge is never wholly lost throughout life.

In our language, then, we have words that point to agreement and others that deny agreement. Words frequently point toward or away from something. But we have many degrees of intensity and we often use them to confuse ourselves. Some of our move-forward words are love, admire, like, friendly, hope, happy, pleased, glad, smiling, enthusiastic, interested, curious, confident, toward, attentive, accepting and others of that ilk. Some of our moving-away-from words are sad, dejected, disappointed, glum, angry, lazy, hostile, depressed, blue, nervous, fearful, timid, hateful, spiteful, apathetic, anxious, resistant, numb, jealous, envious and many more. The importance of *reducing* verbal concepts to an awareness of their yes-no subtleties cannot be overestimated. It prevents one from getting lost in a trap of words, so he may know his direction at all times.

An excellent example of how this works can be seen in the word "anxiety." Anxiety is often thought of as a thing-in-itself—floating free with a mysterious life of its own, like a ghost in search of a house to haunt. But if we translate it into the language of action at the level of the nervous system, we see there is no real difference between anxiety and *hostility*. They are two different words for *the same rejecting movement*! A person who dares not express his hostility openly merely masks or submerges it; it then appears as anxiety. Thus he can remain at a distance from the situation, which is precisely what he wants to do.

Another example of confusion is seen in the comment of a person who remarked, "If someone does me wrong, I always forgive them—but I never forget!" In short, the "Good I" gloats in opulent self-righteousness, while the

"Bad Me" efficiently goes about the business of eviscerating his enemies.

Such examples can be multiplied indefinitely. But all that is important for us to realize is that it is easy to invent and play games at the language level that will not work out at all when we face the neuromuscular level of activity. We must watch both levels—our mouth and our feet—at all times to see what is happening. Then, as in all other psychological problems, the resolution lies in accepting full responsibility for *all that is happening on both levels*!

If we watch only movement, as Adler suggested, we cannot be fooled by others, nor can we any longer fool ourselves. What a person does is what he truly means.

# 14 / *Main tent vs side shows*

This chapter might be sub-titled Problems of Addiction. Addictions are nothing incomprehensible or mysterious. They are merely ways of evading demands of everyday life. The nature and intensity of our evasion is in direct ratio to the demand and our fear of meeting it. Addictions are designed to provide an alibi for not facing what is demanded of us by life; they provide an escape. In this way, we can avoid the threat of confronting an image of ourselves we don't want to see and, at the same time, maintain an appearance that we accept. Our image in our own eyes must appear to be on the side of the angels.

Alcoholism is a good example of a side-show activity. Compulsive, irresistible drinking usually begins around thirty-five and often stops after sixty. It has no *cause*; it only has the purpose of providing a hypersensitive person with an anodyne for his easily hurt feelings and an alibi for avoiding situations in which he fears his prestige may be damaged. Side shows, then, are always for the purpose of avoiding humiliation in the outside world by some genuine, confronting problem. In the side show, we substitute a self-inflicted defeat, like alcoholism, to save our sense of face.

It is important to understand the basic demands of life if we hope to understand the various kinds of evasions we conjure up to dodge them. Alfred Adler pointed out that there are three basic problems each of us faces. What a person actually does about these confronting problems is his real answer to them; not what he says about them or what he thinks he should do about them. It is the latter that is the basis for his neurotic evasions. *Should, ought* and *must* hide behind evasions.

The three problems are *sex, association* and *work*. We are born male and female and must face this fact in love and marriage. Survival depends on living in some close group, family or association with each other. Man is obliged by physical necessity to cooperate on a basis of mutuality, or else on some dominance-submission level. Man must have artificial clothing, shelter, tools, education and endless other goods as well as services to protect him. By means of the division of labor, each man can choose a skill that suits him best and make it the basis for his contribution. By the exchange of goods for goods, each participates as an independent producer in the world around him and is able to get what he needs for himself in return for what he gives to the group. What a person does—or fails to do—is his true answer to each of these three problems.

It is easily seen that evasions can be tailored by the individual to fit the situation being evaded in any one, or in all three, of these areas. The only basis, however, on which any continuing relationship can survive is on a live-and-let-live cooperative one, in balance—based on mutual profit. A relationship based on exploitation—in which one habitually takes more than his share—eventually destroys itself, as with a cancer and its host.

Mutual advantage is *not an ideal*; it is enforced by our basic inability to survive physically on our own efforts alone, like a germ or yeast plant. The whole purpose of education in any society should be aimed at preparing individuals to understand these three problems and to help them develop their attitudes and skills to be able to contribute to, and thus feel *equal to*, those around them. Otherwise they can never be self-reliant and able to fulfill their basic role in life. They can only wish, whine, complain and beg to get along.

As we have seen, the desire for personal recognition or to be the favorite child makes one hostile and puts one at cross-purposes to this performance that must go on endlessly in the main tent of life. The flight into side-show activities is easily understood in this light. We are mistakenly trained, allowed and encouraged to compete against each other for favor and recognition. We are led to believe that life is a race and that we must win out over all others. If we cannot dominate, outfight and outrun them, we lose face and shamefully seek to evade the main tent by inventing our own side-show activity—closer to our heart's ideal desire.

Adler pointed out that the proper training formula and the goal of the emotionally free individual should be: "Life means us to be a help and not a burden." A man is valuable and secure in this world only to the extent that he is not distracted by competitive ambition (envy) and is able to turn his interest freely to productive, constructive activity that gives him a legitimate place in the exchange of goods for goods that must go on in the main tent.

One of the most important factors to understand is the compulsion, or drive (habit), that grows out of our partially conscious goal of expectations. The emotional difficulties we suffer in life arise out of our unrealistic demands and ideal expectations. They do not arise, as many believe, from the reality of daily life in the main tent. The pain we suffer is only the pain we created by *our resistance* to the live-and-let-live demands in the main tent. Pain arises from the intensity of our resistance to, or rejection of, confronting circumstance; we do not want to deal with the live-and-let-live demands on a matter-of-fact basis.

Every confronting situation is measured by us to see whether it favors or threatens the achievement of our goal of ideal expectations. But the main tent of everyday life is wholly different than we expected; it is indifferent to our ideal demands for special privilege. It is a smorgasbord. We may take only what it provides—if we pay for it. There is no mother in the kitchen, as used to be the case at home, to cook special dishes for a special appetite. An abundant opportunity lies before our eyes. If a person looks at that, and still feels deprived and disappointed, it is because his expectancy is bigger than his stomach for reality. The perfectionist is doomed to starve in the midst of plenty. He will resist and reject What Is—simply because it can never measure up to his imagined goal of what-should-be.

Here is the area of conflict. When the greedy eyes of a child look on the smorgasbord of reality, the feeling of being deprived and thwarted arises. And the feeling of rebellion also arises, especially when we must pay for what we get. This leads to a vicious circle. The more we expect, the sooner we are disappointed; the sooner we are disappointed, the more we want. And around we go! But life is wholly impartial, and eventually this vicious circle becomes a descending spiral. The more we demand and need, the less we get. Then follows a flight into the side show of unreality. The bugle blows—and we made an "advance toward the rear." We develop a side show to *explain,* or alibi, why we no longer function on a matter-of-fact basis in the main tent. It becomes our wooden leg to display in the side show as a plea for special privilege—a desire to be excused from the price *others* are expected to pay for things, a desire for bargain prices, a fire sale!

The person who is trapped in this kind of a revolving door must realize, if he is to stop going around and around, that there is *only one* point-of-reference he can change in any way. He cannot change the way the world is made. Nor can he change what has happened in his childhood. It is past forever. Certainly, discussing it will not alter it. Nor can he change the idle, mischievous fantasies he invents in the side show as a way of licking his wounds from encounters with what happens in the main tent. The *one point* open to him for change is that he is *free to alter his wishful thinking—his expectancy.*

You cannot change the world except to the extent you change yourself. It is your move! You cannot change other people. They are as they are. You can change yourself, however, *only* to the degree you alter, modify or become aware of your unrealistic ideal expectations of what-should-be. It is the what-should-be that bars the gate to reality. *You and you alone can change your fate.*

The person who wants to help himself must be willing

# CHART V: MAIN TENT VS SIDE SHOWS

*Side-show Activities*

- Area of illusion and wishes
- Fantasy and ideal solutions
- Seduction from reality—abdication, perfectionism, neurosis, addiction, feeling of weakness and criminality

*Goal of Ideal Expectations*

- Ambition for personal recognition
- Dreams of greatness
- Wish to be favored child
- Itch to rule, dominate, exploit, influence and use others for personal satisfaction

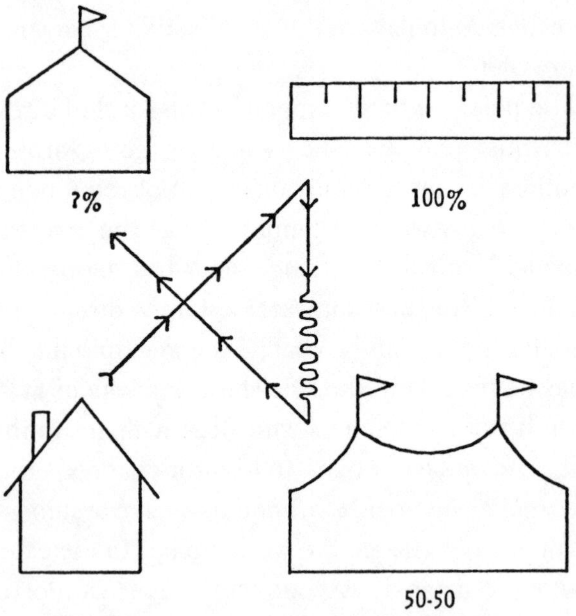


*Childhood Situation*

- Position of weakness and inadequacy vis-a-vis world
- Projection of fantasy expectations and ideal compensations

*Main Tent—The What Is of Living Now*

- Mutual advantage and productivity
- Cooperation—live and let live
- Spend self—pay as you go
- No special privilege
- "To Be a Help and Not a Burden"

to see that all his trouble arises out of his ideal expectations and not, as he thought, from the main tent, the side show or from his childhood. Waste no time blaming your parents, the evil world or the terrible addiction you may have chosen as a companion. Nothing that happened and nothing anyone does to you is *to blame for what you do*! What you do comes out of your mistaken ideal of what life ought to be according to your imagination.

To understand that difficulties grow out of mistaken ideal expectations is to see why it is useless for the alcoholic to fight his thirst, the drug addict to fight his craving, the thief to fight his desire to steal, and similar side-show activities. In Zen, it is said that it is "useless to try to wash off blood with blood." Such side-show activities will not go away until we destroy our mistaken expectations—our demand for special recognition. Only then will we stop trying to treat the symptom, which is nothing more than the futile effort to enhance our damaged significance. As it says in the New Testament: "Ye pray, and your prayers are not answered, because ye pray amiss!" No Providence can give that which is beyond the What Is of the eternal now.

# 15 / *Alienation from the here-and-now*

Our life has been described as a spark of light between two towering walls of darkness. There is no past and no tomorrow; they are figments of the imagination. It is always and eternally now. But the mind is subject to the dangerous illusion that we can project ourselves outside the present reality, outside the eternal now, and thus escape any present pain by fleeing into some ideal expectation. All flight into the ideal, the should be, the ought-to-be, is illusion. All illusion is alienation from the now.

An alien is a person living in a country not his own, without rights of citizenship. The person who rejects, and thus is alienated from, the now has abdicated his native inherited abilities to flee into another country, one of wishes, dreams and ideals, which exists somewhere over the rainbow of wishful thinking. The perfectionist, the idealist and the reformer are examples of those who have cut ties with the living now and aimlessly wander, like the Flying Dutchman, going nowhere, adrift at sea.

Life is being. And *all being is now*. Life cannot be postponed nor transposed. Alienation from reality, in its extreme degree, is psychosis—a flight from reality into dreams and fancy.

Our degree of alienation—or distance from the living now—is in direct ratio to our habit of wishful thinking. Wishes are the fool's gold that tempt us into alienating ourselves from the now. They send us in search of the illusion of greatness, the illusion of progress and success—or the desire to make a big impression!

Curiously enough, alienation from the now is similar to a defective clutch that slips in a car. Instead of meshing gears, as a clutch is designed to do, it slips out and idles. While it is in neutral, the car and driver are not related to the confronting traffic situation. Nothing happens. Similarly, if we lose our hold on the now, we slip into idling dreams and are not related to the confronting life situation. Life is an emerging thing, much like oncoming traffic. The function of the human psyche is to meet such situations and be an active part of them, just as a driver must thread his way through on-coming traffic. Life has no place for victims who ignore this changing pattern of on-coming traffic, because they are driving with blinders in search of greatness.

Physical and emotional self-reliance is possible only as long as we are fully planted in the present. The problems of life demand response and activity. Any evasion of the now is a way of trying to postpone activity. If we *abdicate our initiative*, we become passive-receptive victims of on-coming circumstances. This effort to escape the now by a flight into ideals, dreams, expectations or hopes can be called living on the deferred-payment plan; that is, we promise ourselves rewards tomorrow. We say to ourselves that we will begin to have courage and to live tomorrow—we dare not live today! But this is a world of the eternal now; there is no tomorrow. The result is that we are alienated from life entirely. We are incapable of living either now or tomorrow.

Dreams or illusions avoid, postpone and abort action. That which destroys action destroys life. Each of us must consciously choose between two ways of facing life: we must (1) live in direct, spontaneous contact with the emerging now or (2) live fearfully on the deferred-payment plan as an alien from reality in a world of wishful thinking, ideal expectancy and endless searching. There is no middle ground; there are no shades of gray between. The choice is uncompromising.

The Biblical story of the creation and the fall of man points to the same two choices. Alienation is based on the

## THE TWO WORLDS OF BEING AND BECOMING

**BEING**

*This Is It! Reality*

- Nothing to achieve
- Nothing to get
- Nothing to seek
- Nothing to prove
- Nowhere to go
- No big brother checking on us
- No head higher than our own

**BECOMING**

*The Illusion of Progress! Wishes*

- Ambition—desire for personal recognition
- The begging attitude—"Please love me"
- Degrading dependence on approval of others
- Feeling of emptiness—emotional poverty
- Treadmill of endless search for rewards
- Dancing for pay—outside approval
- Living on the deferred-payment-plan—living on empty hopes of future bentfits—the abdication from the living now

illusion of becoming. The Devil is known as the father of lies and illusions. "If ye eat of this fruit," he promised Eve, "ye too shall become as gods, knowing good from evil." In other words, you can stop being a producer and sit above others, finding fault with them. That is, instead of performing deeds, you can occupy yourself with the appearances of things.

Daydreams are one of the costliest disaster areas known to man. Extreme fantasy is schizophrenia; most of the beds in mental hospitals are filled with unfortunates who abdicated the now for dreams of grandeur. What we call insanity begins when we are no longer willing to distinguish clearly between the world of what happens and what-we-wish-were-true! The majority of us, unfortunately, usually run a zig-zag course between these two worlds.

We mistakenly seek false-compensation solutions to our problems. We want to be free of them. We desire to escape from confronting situations without bothering to understand them, the way a chicken flies a coop. But we cannot fly above the bars put up against reality by our wishful thinking. It is our vain ambition for recognition, not reality, that traps and enslaves us.

We want to escape and to live like a worm in an apple, without effort or pain. Our aversion to pain is in fact the basic source of our pain. Psychological pain does not arise from the level of What Is. Pain lies in our *effort to resist pain.* Pain-pleasure are but two inseparable ends of the same stick. We can't pick up one end of the stick without the other coming along. Our effort to grasp one end without the other leads to our resistance. It is a case of wanting to know good without evil. But the now is neither good nor bad. It is all that there is.

# 16 / *It isn't polite to point*

When we complain about what someone is doing that annoys us, we are really not complaining about him at all. We are complaining about our *own character*. We make a fuss about what he is doing, but that is useless as he will probably keep right on doing it. Instead of being annoyed about what he is doing, we ought to be more interested in finding out the answer to a vital question: "*Why does it bother me?*"

Another person's behavior is probably his usual manner of relating to his environment. Whether it is adequate or defective, from our point of view, isn't the issue. He has probably been that way for years. Certainly there is nothing we can do to change him, and he probably isn't going to change just to please us either. If any changes are to be made, the one who does the complaining is the one who has to change.

What is wrong with me if I find myself annoyed by what you are doing? If I point the finger of blame at you, there are three other long fingers on that same hand and all three are pointing straight back at me! What weakness exists in me that I can't endure what you are doing? If you can stand it, why can't I? It is up to me to examine and change my own weakness. You are not obliged to improve your character just to make the world less annoying for me. It is obvious that others are not about to improve their behavior either just so that I can escape improving my own behavior.

There is the story of the Oriental potentate who complained that the rough ground hurt his feet. He ordered his whole kingdom to be carpeted with cowhide to protect his feet when he went walking. But his chief adviser pointed out the difficulty of carpeting the whole kingdom; he suggested they cut out small pads of cowhide to cover each of the potentate's feet instead. If we can't eliminate all the rough behavior of other people, then we must find a way *to protect ourselves from our irritability* without demanding that they change.

We might as well assume, for our own comfort and convenience, the point of view that "the other fellow never makes mistakes." For what I complain about is my own personal difficulty, or inability, to endure what he is doing. Not everyone objects to him! It is my own defective self-reliance that is the true source of pain to me—not what he is doing. Whether the other fellow is ethically, morally or legally right must not be the main consideration. If I want to challenge each person who annoys me and demand he change to suit me, I shall spend my life in lawsuits against man and the gods.

We do not see things as *they are*. The fact is that we see things as *we are*! We read our own wishes and bias into what we see. It is of no use to say, "I wouldn't do that to anyone; why does he do it to me?" The only answer to such a question is, "He does what he does because that is his way of doing things." That is the way he is, and he is not about to change to make me happy. I had better say, "Why do I expect so much of him? Why am I so lacking in self-reliance—and why do I lean on him so much? What could I be doing instead of fighting him and his ways if I were more self-reliant?"

Very few of us would give our credit card to a comparative stranger and expect him to use it wisely and for our good! Why, then, do we place our welfare and contentment on the back of someone, often a total stranger, and expect him to handle us with tender, loving care? It is not the responsibility of the other fellow to look after our welfare or happiness. When we stop expecting that he will do so, then we shall not have any complaint against him *if he does not do so*. We have no right to feel emotionally hurt or damaged at what seems to be the inconsiderate behavior of those around us. They are what they are—not what we wish them to be, to suit our purpose. If we are not leaning on them, then they cannot let us down!

All the mistakes that we bitterly complain about, then, are really projections of our own mistakes that grow out of our own lack of self-sufficiency. We may not excuse ourselves for lacking self-reliance by blaming someone else because he does not take care of us for our advantage. If I feel damaged, it is my mess and I must clean it up myself. This is an imperfect world, filled with imperfect situations and imperfect people. And I am one of them—a fact I share with all others. My complaints against others only draw their attention to the manner in which I am leaning on them for their support. And blaming them when they do not freely give it to me. It is not polite to point! Worse still, we expose our own nakedness in public when we do. No one would know a peacock cannot sing if it only had sense enough to keep its mouth shut!

# 17 / *Death by sweet talk*

The most important job each of us has is to keep his personal initiative intact at all times so as not to be touted off by outside forces. One of the greatest temptations we have to face is the trap set by praise and its dark twin —blame.

Few of us are wholly desensitized to the seductive music of praise. Most people eagerly snatch at and swallow even a few words of praise, as a starving dog grabs at a piece of steak. For most of us, praise has the intoxicating effect of alcohol on an empty stomach. A warm flush spreads over us as we throw our initiative out the window and madly pursue the Pied Piper of approval for every remaining crumb of praise. We may become the willing slave of anyone who continues to pour forth additional libations for us. We drool, we posture, we grovel, we pant—and we beg for more. We are flattered and the truth is no longer in us. We remain the helpless tool of anyone who is willing to pet and pander us gently.

The more a person becomes addicted to praise, the more vulnerable he becomes to the chills of blame. The dependent adult wants an approving world with never a shadow of disapproval. Thus he finds himself trapped by his addiction to approval. Like a lost dog at a parade, he runs in search of someone who will pat him on the head.

The tragedy of the praise-addicted individual is similar to that of the alcoholic or drug addict, because his initiative has been lost to outside forces he cannot control. The praise-dependent person is trapped in a helpless dither. He is caught between the desire to snatch at the bait of praise and the fear of being caught on the barb of blame. There is always a hook hidden in the bait of praise. The tongue of the person who praises us is forked like a snake's. The tongue that can lift us up with praise can just as easily cut us down with blame. The person who feels free to praise us is just as free to blame us when it suits his purpose.

Why are we so vulnerable to this seemingly magical power that lies in praise? Why do we seem to be so defenseless to its sound? The answer is not far away;

sounds like the old, remembered voice of our parental authority-figures still seem to manipulate us and influence us, now as then. We remember these voices all too well, and we remember our dependence on them, as children, for approval of our aims. Disapproval brought swift punishment.

We are no longer children, but we may still have the habit of seeking support, benefits and contentment from outside ourselves by trying to entice and captivate other people. We can never hope to be free of this vulnerability to praise-blame until and unless we *give up putting other heads higher than our own*! The self-sufficient person is in no danger of being seduced or intimidated by praise or blame, since he is leaning on no one else and thus can't be lifted up or let down by them.

Our parents used praise and blame as a way to control us as children. Rewards were given for obedience or submission—and punishment was given if we resisted their domination. The memory of such experiences is burned deeply into our nervous system. We respond automatically to such conditioning. Both the desire to submit obediently and to win praise is so habitual that it acts as an unconscious compulsion. Old conditioning of the nervous system cannot be erased; it is like nail holes in boards. It is possible, however, to minimize the dangerous conditioning of praise and blame. Praise is a weapon for domination. We use it to seek power over unwary victims and fear it unconsciously when it is used on us.

What is less clear to many is that the goal of blame is exactly the same as the goal of praise; its target is domination. If we cannot seduce our intended victim with praise, we use blame to frighten him into the trap.

It is important at all times for an individual to be aware at which level of manipulation he is operating. Am I the one who is praising (using praise to influence) or am I the one who is being praised (to be influenced)? In other words, am I the hunter or the hunted! In both cases, of course, there is larceny in the heart of the hunter as well as in the heart of the hunted, if he is susceptible to the blandishment and hungry for the bait. You cannot cheat an honest man.

There is another interesting facet to the business of praise and blame. It can be twisted to serve the purpose of self-glorification. Praise someone extravagantly and you oblige him to scratch your back in return, which is why you do what you do to get support from others. Or you can belittle yourself extravagantly, and the other person feels obliged to come to your defense and lift you up above the blows you seem to be raining on your own apparently defenseless head. In both instances, the object is to trap the other fellow to scratch your back for you.

Another aspect of this subtle trap is the hidden but

more purely self-laudatory use of praise or blame. The person who praises or blames another has set himself up above others as a superior person in an elevated position from where he can pass judgments down on those beneath him. If I express admiration for the cut of your coat, I am saying behind my hand: "You lucky man! Your taste in coats is almost, but not quite, as good as my own." This type of praise—if it is rightly understood—is more like a slap in the face. It can be a way of belittling and patronizing the one we praise. We are, in a sense, spitting on his head. Or he on ours. At the best, we form a mutual-admiration society. Neither dares accuse the other of having bad taste.

The most pathetic use of praise and blame is when we praise someone out of envy for his abilities. Any performer who has been able to build up admiration for his ability attracts fan clubs that glorify his name. The fans want to be near the star performer in the hope that some of his fame will rub off on them. But, as Adler said: "No one likes to look up all the time; it makes the back of his neck tired." The person who is a fan both hates and loves his idol; he approaches to get from, and not to give to, his idealized figure, who simultaneously impresses and oppresses him. The whole tragedy of hero worship is that we want to occupy the position of the idol, but it stands in our way. Eventually, we knock him down from the elevation we have given him in our imagination to elevate ourself. This is the fever—the ferment of the envious mind.

We must conclude that all praise and blame is evidence of the habit of making *envious comparisons*. It shows how we alienate ourselves from our own initiative by putting other heads higher than our own. The only antidote, or safeguard, we can use against such envy is matter-of-factness. Sweet talk is begging talk—and should be left for children.

# *18 / Need or greed?*

What is the difference between need and greed? Or is there a basic difference at all? Is need a continuum which imperceptibly turns into greed? Like white that goes through shades of gray until it is pure black? Is it possible to tell whether we really needed that extra drink or bite of food, the more expensive suit, the new shoes and all those things?

It is almost impossible to get agreement among people as to what constitutes *human needs* and what lies outside them. It is difficult to find a common standard by which to judge. But at the psychological level no such problem exists. Psychological need and psychological greed are worlds apart! They grow out of wholly different soil. At the psychological level, we are dealing with expectations and feelings—not with tangibles. What we *feel that we need* does not necessarily have any relation to what we *truly need*—or even what is good for us. They can come together or they can be miles apart.

At the psychological level, we are not dealing with reality *per se*. We are on the level of *feeling* and how we *view* a situation. At this level, we discover that two separate worlds exist, and each has laws and internal consistency all its own. We discover there is the feeling of fullness and the feeling of poverty.

The feeling of poverty is bottomless; it cannot be satisfied by any amount of accumulation, possessions or achievement. There is no compensation for it. Any effort to kill desire by accumulation or achievement only stimulates greater ambition to achieve and possess. The situation is similar to the shipwrecked sailor on a raft who tries to quench his thirst by drinking sea water. The more he drinks, the sooner he will die, as it only draws the existing water out of his bloodstream.

On the other hand, the feeling of fullness is independent of what we have or don't have. It is such that we feel adequate in all situations, so that we do not need to get, achieve, grasp, steal, possess or take from anyone. We are in full contact with the world around us and function without a sense of strain. We are filled to capacity with the here-and-now. We seek nothing outside ourselves.

Nothing can fill the void of the feeling of poverty because it is not based on lack; it is the shadow cast by habitual comparison and envy. Mirror, mirror in my hand, who is the fairest in the land? The feeling of poverty, then, does not arise from any realistic need we have. For this reason, it can never be compensated for by any real achievements on our part. While we are envious, the feeling of poverty continues, though we may be rich as kings.

The feeling of fullness, or adequacy, on the other hand, exists when one's center-of-gravity is inside a person and he does not lean, depend on, or expect from, those around him. When one gives up comparing and seeking to enrich himself through others, he gives up seeking fulfillment *outside himself*. He makes no further efforts to extort happiness from others by using them for his satisfactions. When he is no longer tempted to turn outside himself to make others responsible for his own welfare, he finally comes to rest within himself.

# 19 / *Aloneness is not loneliness*

Many people are not aware of the real difference between aloneness and loneliness. They mistakenly believe they are two words for the same condition. It is very important to understand these two conditions inasmuch as they are worlds apart. Aloneness is the basis of our greatest strength; loneliness is a sign of our greatest weakness. Aloneness is the mark of emotional maturity. Loneliness is the unmistakable stamp of the immature.

Loneliness is the emptiness felt by a leaning, dependent individual when he has no one on whom to lean for comfort, entertainment or support. The dependent person has not learned how to occupy himself in any interesting, productive manner. He seeks someone who will amuse, divert, distract and reassure him, so that he will not become aware of his inability to face the world alone. In short, he seeks a baby-sitter. He has not trained himself to invent activity of his own, to build, to make or to discover, explore and improvise in the world around him. He seeks someone to take him by the hand and lead him into greener pastures of enjoyment. When he can find no one who will make him the center of their support and attention, he comes into contact with a deep and abiding loneliness.

Such individuals usually find it difficult to establish any enduring relationships. Because they are so nonproductive and shallow in their lives, others find them boring companions and avoid them when possible. They demand so much and give back so little. As a result, they are thrown back upon themselves, which reinforces their loneliness. But since they lack the basic amount of self-reliance, their situation does not improve.

Aloneness, on the other hand, is very much like the stars coming out at night. We are unaware of our inner voice while our ears are filled with the clatter of outside voices—just as we are unable to see the stars at noon because of the sun's glare. The mature individual has learned to close his ears to conflicting voices outside himself and to listen to the sound of his own inner world.

Aloneness is the independent inner life when we have finally shut our ears to the competing voices of those who wish to influence us and our own desire to influence them in turn. When we have let go of our own possessiveness, our desire to compete, dominate and exploit, our need for personal recognition and the other remnants of our childhood, then the inner voice is quite clear and a whole world opens up inside us. Everything comes to life and has a nature of its own. We can see directly into it without any desire to distort, improve, modify or change the outside world at all. We can see it for what it really is, without any stardust in our eyes to blind us.

Aloneness, then, is a fullness of spirit and knows no feeling of want or poverty. Fullness is complete. Loneliness is the empty world of seeking for outside fires to warm us. It is the child who has lost his parents in a crowd and is terrified by his lack of knowing what to do. It is strange that two words that sound so much alike should point to such vastly different situations. Only by examining them at the action level can we truly know what happens.

# 20 / *Psychological memory*

Psychological memory is a special kind of remembering that is endlessly destructive. It is a specially trained habit some of us have for remembering old grudges, old humiliations, insults to our pride, threats to our prestige and rivalries. Where this habit clouds the mind, there is only darkness, slavery, suspicion and a pall of fear.

We become injustice collectors. We collect and cherish hurt feelings as though they were priceless works of art. We cling jealously to all things anyone has ever said or done to us that in any way seems to detract from our image of ourself in our own eyes. We are not content merely to collect these acts of commission and omission seemingly made against us; we insist on going further. We build up grudges about what we think they may be thinking against us.

Some people seem to enjoy this imagined kind of insult even better than the real ones in their collection! This accumulation of real and imaginary insults constitutes psychological memory.

We keep this memory keen by making a rosary out of our grudges, and we go over each bead endlessly, remembering the particular insult it represents for us! What pleasure! It makes us feel so virtuous to be so crucified by the unworthy and the unwashed who crushed us with the unkindness. We rehearse the emotions and scenes associated with the insult that each bead represents and the shame of being put back or put down. Repeated intoning of the beads builds up a killing rage within us and the feeling of being the martyred saint. Thus we destroy our perspective on ourself and all those we have been condemning in the process. We make them look like monsters so we can attack and destroy them eventually. In short, this is the direct path to paranoia.

Grudges, like animals in a zoo, must be fed daily. If we do not revive them in our memory and water them with our tears, they perish. The practiced grudge collector isn't out of bed in the morning before he has picked up his rosary and begun his endless rounds on it. His greatest fear is that he will lose a bead and have less to feel put back about. He won't part with a single one of them.

Why does he fear to forget a single grudge when he has so many of them? Blaming others is an easy way to build up the feeling of our own importance, so that we can console ourselves for not making a bigger splash in the outside world. It is an easy way to feel that we are big shots that are being overlooked. Blaming others gives us a fictitious elevation. It allows us to look down on others.

Not many of us are entirely free of the habit of blaming others and holding grudges. Psychological memory is a curse to most of us. But if we listen to our voice blaming, condemning, judging, belittling others, we soon become nauseated with our own holier-than-thou pretense of moral superiority, and we soon become allergic to our own big-me and little-you posture. Self-praise stinks, and we can't stand our own variety. It soon produces instant nausea as an antidote to our habit of injustice collecting, so that we are happy to see the end of it.

# 21 / *Reconditioning old habits*

By now, the reader is probably wondering how he is going to free himself of old conditioning that is making trouble for him. The old problem of will power comes to mind; we begin to think of ways that we can administer self-discipline in a hope that we can force ourselves to give up the offending habit. But the first point to realize is that one cannot free his mind of an old habit by efforts of will power and discipline. That is like one hand wrestling against the other.

It is not possible to give up anything we regard as desirable. When the official statement was made that cigarettes were definitely dangerous to health, the sale dropped sharply because many people stopped smoking. But they suffered great discomforts from the feeling of being deprived. They had no desire to give up smoking, and their mind was filled with the longing to return to their old friend, a cigarette. The more they fought against the desire, the more conscious of the desire they became, until it overwhelmed them and they began to smoke again.

We cannot give up anything *against our inner wish*. As long as it seems desirable to us, our old habits, like an old bird dog, will find a way to bring it to us. *No amount of will power is of the slightest use* in giving up old habits.

This fact is well known to those who have given up drinking in Alcoholics Anonymous. The alcoholic has to be in such pain that he is willing to do anything, even get well! He has to be thoroughly disenchanted with alcohol and what it does for him. He has to know that there is no way for him to drink even a small amount of alcohol without going on to the bitter end. He must know every aspect of his enemy. He has to see the whole wasteland alcohol makes for him in daily life. He has to see it so clearly that he sees he is not giving up an old, delightful companion. On the contrary, he is *getting rid* of a curse. He is ditching a bad companion and happy to see the last of it.

*Getting rid of something we dislike* is quite a different

thing to us than *giving up something we like.* This probably stems from the acquisitive, possessive habit we originally had as children. Every parent knows that if you want to take something away from a baby, you have to offer the baby something else with the other hand. It is much the same with us; we resist any kind of surrender if we interpret it as *being deprived of a want*! But we gladly get rid of a pin that is sticking us! Everything seems to depend on the value judgment we make about a habit. And we can do nothing about a habit unless we change the value judgment and put the habit in another context. It all depends on how you look at it!

Now just how is this going to get us out of a bind when we are trapped? A bind, as we have learned before, is made up of equal parts of ambition and caution; we want to go both ways at once! The way to get out of a bind is to *allow yourself to be in the bind.*

In short, the person who is afraid of stage fright must *give himself permission* to be as scared as he may get. He must be willing to forget his lines and to stand there with his mind a blank while he sweats and trembles! He must be willing to stand there and *watch* himself sweat and tremble just as long as it continues—without doing anything to break the spell of fear upon him. He must be willing to let go at any price and *see what happens.* He must stand there as if he were watching a child at play. But he must do it without making any value judgments about what is happening or what may happen to him in the process. It is as if he were swimming and let himself do the dead man's float.

Does this seem too great a price to pay? But only the meek shall inherit the earth, it is said. It is our pride, our need for personal recognition that builds the trap. And *it is only when we let go of the demand for recognition that we can get out of the trap. We are our only jailor*! There is no one outside ourself who is holding us in a bind.

To let go and walk on is the way of living in the here-and-now; one may not hold on. To hold on, means to hold on to our need for recognition, our pride, our dependence on the opinions of those around us and what we believe they think of us. We are prisoners of the *value judgments* of other people, and until we get rid of them, we cannot be free to function in the now. We must practice the art of nonattachment!

How does one achieve nonattachment and the freedom it brings from value systems? That is not as difficult as it may sound. Each of us, as an individual, must learn to know himself in a nonjudgmental way! We have to learn to look at our total behavior without any form of pride or humiliation about what we see. We may not enjoy or dislike what we see. We must merely know the What Is of our own behavior. As Adler said, "If you want to understand yourself or another person, close your ears to anything that is said or what you think and watch only movement. What a person does is his real understanding and intention."

We have only to watch our footsteps, then. There is a tongue in each shoe and a tongue in our head. The tongue in our head tries to tell the truth but too often talks ideas, ideals, shoulds and oughts! It lies without our knowing it is lying. But we have only to listen to the tongues in our shoes and ask them which way we are, or have been, going. They never lie; they are never confused about which way they are pointing at any given moment. A sailor at sea checks his course by the stars and compass as he sails out of sight of land. He cannot trust his guesses. We must check our movement by our feet.

To change a habit, then, we must look at ourselves dispassionately while our feet are acting according to their dictates. Condemning bad habits only serves to fasten our hold on them when we make an effort to suppress them. When we push down on them they merely push right back at us. The feeling of guilt only gives the habit a stronger hold on us. Adler used to say, "Either do wrong or feel guilty, but don't do both; it is too much work!" It is not surprising, then, that an alcoholic can't stop drinking as long as he feels guilty and condemns himself as a weakling for not having the strength of character to stop drinking. His guilt only makes him feel inferior and makes the next drink more necessary to help forget the insult.

We must develop in ourselves the habit of total nonjudgmental awareness of everything we are doing. If you are against smoking but find yourself with a cigarette in your hand, sit passively by and watch yourself light it, cough, put out the match, drop ashes on yourself—and every move you make. At the same time, listen to yourself saying to yourself how you ought to give up smoking for your health's sake and what a weak character you are, smoking in spite of high resolves to quit.

If you do this for a while, you will become aware of a curious thing. It is almost as if you sat in a room where two sound recorders, or TV sets, were playing two different programs at the same time but using the same cast of characters in the plot. Or it may seem like the old Western dramas with good guys and bad guys fighting it out. You will observe that you habitually pit the two sides against each other—the ideal image which is on the side of the angels against the What Is of your everyday behavior, which is a bad guy most of the time.

The process just described is the way we bring *unconscious habit* into the spotlight of total awareness. The double bind is only possible in those areas where unconscious habit is leading us astray. We cannot escape the pitfall of an unconscious habit as long as it remains at that level of nonawareness. It behaves as if it were a compulsion to drink, smoke, eat, kill or you-name-it. We are mystified and baffled by the blind power that seems to drive us to our destruction quite against our conscious will. It is vital for us to know the meaning of unconscious habit and the role that it plays in creating the double bind that traps us.

Under no circumstance should this concept of unconscious habit be identified with what is sometimes called the unconscious. The unconscious is a theoretical invention of Freud, and it is supposed to house the part of the soul, or psyche, that is *hidden to our own conscious observation! Unconscious habit* is nothing at all like that! *We are quite aware of its presence in our lives.* We see it plainly and others can see it, too. What is unconscious about it is the *mistaken significance we give it.* It is our lack of understanding of the role the unconscious habit plays that baits the trap!

No one of us is unaware of trying to make a good impression or of striving for personal recognition. Or of making invidious comparisons between ourselves and those around us. These are unconscious habits, nevertheless. They can continue to trip us up just as long as we are not wholly aware that such activity on our part is the root of our own destruction. I shall not be willing to give up enviously comparing myself with others so long as I feel it helps me to get my due in life. But when I finally see with total awareness that it leads to my own destruction, I gladly get rid of it as fast as possible.

William James said that forming a new habit is like winding string on a ball. The longer we wind without dropping it, the better. If it drops and rolls, we have that much more to wind back on the ball again. Finally, the new habit is strong enough to go by itself, so that the temptation to fall back into the old one is less compelling. But the alcoholic knows that old habits are like old generals; they never die.

There is only one way. When we realize finally that we are not bound by our past, we are magically free of it and we can let go of all regrets, recriminations and alibis based on it. We have nothing to hide or to defend. Our mind is free to be wholly in the here-and-now, to deal with confronting circumstances as they arise for our attention. What has happened in the past is forever dead and we have nothing to do except to *play by ear as we go along.* We can let the dead bury the dead as it should be. And the old conditioning of the past comes to an end.

# BEYOND SUCCESS AND FAILURE / II

# *Food for thought*

» COMPARISONS

Comparisons breed fear and fear breeds comparisons. Fear and comparisons, in turn, breed competition. Our language reports these relationships as if they could exist as separate things or on a one-at-a-time basis. But that is a limitation of language. In reality, they coexist and are never found separately any more than you could have an inside without an outside. If we are aware of only having one of these attributes and imagine we are free of the others, we are deluding ourselves. We have the total infection and must pay the total price of this costly package. They are only different aspects of the same evil—the leaning, dependent habit of mind.

## » COMPLAINTS

All complaints, in the final analysis, are complaints against one's own character! We should not be filled with righteous indignation about what someone is doing to us. There is small chance that we can stop him from doing it anyhow; that is probably his habitual way of responding in similar situations and he is not about to change it to make us happy.

On the contrary, our main concern should be to find out why it is that what he is doing bugs us! In short, what is the hole in our character through which it can get to us so easily? What defect exists in us that makes his action such a threat to us?

## » PERFECTIONISM

The perfectionist is a frightened, competitive individual who wants always to win and be secure. He mistakenly believes that he is a lover of the truth for its own sake. But the reality is that he only wants to be above criticism and, therefore, superior to those who are less perfect. He is constantly comparing himself with others. He feels exposed to danger if any error is allowed to creep into his own activity. He is seldom aware of his hostile downgrading of those whom he regards as less perfect than he; he belittles their standards and their personal value in order to exalt his own.

The perfectionist is a faultfinder, and nothing is ever good enough for him. He disrupts situations by his belittling of others and disturbs cooperation in a group by trying to exalt and impose his standards on them. He sees only the hole in the doughnut and insists on others condemning it along with him.

The perfectionist loves to collect and tabulate evidence against others to prove their inferiority as human beings and thus put himself in a clear light of superiority. He is proud of his ability to find the Achilles heel and the imperfections of other people—to expose them.

Perfectionism is a side-show activity which destroys the spontaneity and creative power he might otherwise bring to the solution of his own problems. He flees from reality into a search for ideal solutions and thus isolates himself from effective contact with confronting problems; he blinds and deafens himself to the What Is in his illusions of What Should Be.

» CREATION

Creation does not take place in a climate of criticism. Creation is a spontaneous response of the mind—

unpremeditated as a breeze—to some confronting situation. It is a surprise, like an ad-lib retort, or a sudden discovery. It is of the spirit and obeys no law. It springs full born, like Minerva from the brow of Zeus. The process of creation views all avenues as equally enticing and exists in a climate of discovery that is uncritical of exploration.

Criticism is based on comparison, and comparison breeds fear. Any kind of discrimination blocks the path to discovery of the unknown. Criticism is a kind of birth control that prevents the birth of new forms. Gertrude Stein, Picasso and many others would have stopped producing had they been overly critical of their creations in comparison with existing, successful work. Parents would be tempted to destroy their children if they compared them with Apollo and Venus! Fortunately for us, "Every crow regards her chick as the blackest and the best."

There are two kinds of people—creators and haters! Haters hate because they compare, fear and compete. They are faultfinders who boast of their own high ideals and seek to belittle the efforts of others. They are so occupied with being destructive that they have no energy for creating anything of their own.

Creators are lovers. Love laughs at locksmiths. The pleasure and love of the game for its own sake, without reward, unlocks all mysteries; new forms are born out of such uncensored play. Competition is always possessive and ties in knots the mind of the one who engages in it. But real love is always without an object; it has no gain in mind. It has no reward outside itself. Each man has a choice in life; he may approach it as a creator or a competitor, a lover or a hater. One excludes the other. Love, which is without an object, casts out fear!

» BELIEFS

Beliefs obscure and distort reality; they do not reveal it. We cannot see anything outside of a belief; it is self-limiting. A belief is a kind of box, or pen, or frame, which encloses a limited area. No matter how large the pen or frame we build, it inevitably shuts out much more than it can enclose. It ignores that which it shuts out and thus produces what we call ignorance. We see only that which lies safely within the frame.

Beliefs produce what may be called "the framed universe," an island surrounded by the *unframed*, limitless world of reality. A belief is made up of conscious and unconscious information and attitudes that have been given sanction as being valid, coherent and consistent. A belief is definite as well as finite and is bounded by ignorance of anything else that lies outside its frame. To know (believe), then, is really not-to-know but to lean and depend on outside authority. The greatest damage a belief does to one who holds it is that it prevents free exploration, discovery and perception of that limitless world that lies outside the prefabricated truth that is trapped inside the limiting belief. Reality will always elude us and is always greater than any box (belief) we can build to hold it.

People often use the words "faith" and "belief" as synonymous. This is a great mistake. *Faith is everything that belief is not.* Nothing is possible outside a belief to someone who holds that belief. But *with faith, all things are possible.* Belief is static, structured and inflexible. But faith is a condition of wonder and discovery of unknown potentialities which unfold as they are touched. Belief enslaves, faith liberates the individual. Belief knows; faith is a cloud of unknowing, from which new forms emerge.

## » REALITY VS PSEUDO-PROBLEMS

There are two kinds of problems—real problems and pseudo-problems. Real problems seldom give us any enduring, or protracted, difficulties. Those we cannot solve, we either learn to endure or to ignore. An excellent example of a pseudo-problem is the familiar sacred cow—the feeling of rejection! More idle tears have been shed over this pseudo-problem than for any other in the world. All we need to do to get rid of it is to face the fact that no one owes us any duty, honor or support in the first place. We have no right to make demands on them, consciously or otherwise—especially for personal recognition and favor.

Since no one owes us emotional or physical support as a mark of special honor to us, they certainly cannot be accused of withholding or defrauding us of that which they *never owed us in the first place.* We were not rejected by them in any way; we simply didn't belong on their back in the start. It was presumptuous of us to imagine that they were in debt to us and that they had put us down.

Pseudo-problems are inventions of our own mind, not of reality. They can go on for a lifetime, and they stop only when we stop keeping them alive in our mind. The difference between a reality and a pseudo-problem is that the first has a basis in fact but the second comes into being only as a result of making a comparison. Pseudo-problems do not exist apart from our *need for personal recognition.* They grow out of our desire for prestige and our craving to be ahead of all others. As long as I continue to compare myself with someone I imagine to be more fortunate, preferred, or superior, I cannot escape the misery of the inferiority feeling I thus create out of the comparison.

Real problems can be realistically compensated for by some realistic action. Problems we learn to live with do not eat out our heart and lead us to destructive activity. But the contrary is true of pseudo-problems. The individual who believes that all his unhappiness results from having less money than others habitually compares his possessions against those of others around him. This stimulates him to an inner fury and drives him to try to do something to relieve his pain. Sooner or later, he must steal from others or live by some illegal means at the expense of others. Getting things illegally does nothing to relieve the feeling of deprivation, so that the individual must continue on this path.

Pseudo-problems, then, always grow out of competitive comparisons. They are an effort to emulate and keep up with some pacemaker of our choice. Nothing we can do assuages the pain they cause us, and nothing we can do or get relieves us of the problem unless we stop making the comparison that is at the root of the problem. The pain we feel is only the shadow that is cast on the outside world by the comparison we make in our mind, and nothing can erase a shadow—until we remove the thing that casts the shadow.

## » AUTHORITY FIGURES

An authority figure is anything big enough to hide behind for an alibi! Authority figures are merely creations of the human mind; they do not exist outside of it in the realm of reality. They exist only at the psychological level, and we project them as a movie projector throws an image onto a screen. They are only people, but we project them as illusions of authority so that we can use them as an excuse to *abdicate* our personal initiative and personal responsibility. We create them so that we have someone to blame if things go wrong.

We create authority figures exactly as primitive people create idols out of clay and then bow down before them. In both instances, the purpose is the same—to escape personal responsibility and to shift personal initiative from the self to the nonself. We want to regain the original irresponsible situation of dependency, where we can lean on and exploit parent figures. If we achieve emotional self-reliance, we have no temptation to put the heads of other people higher than our own. We see them only as projections of our own imagination.

We must not confuse psychological authority figures with organizational authority figures. Large enterprises in business and governments are so complex that they demand a division of labor and responsibility to accomplish them. The various tasks in each require a variety of skills, and these activities must be coordinated. To achieve a smooth operation, levels and areas of responsibility are mapped to cover all the needs of the operation. Men are placed at each post; each has his own task to do to fit into the total effort. Some supervise the activity of others and some manipulate nonhuman tools, instruments or situations. The president or man at the top level has final responsibility for the activity of all the other men. He is said to have top authority.

This authority is not psychological, and we do not regard the man who holds a top job as a superior being simply because he has a higher level of organizational responsibility. As a matter of fact, outside of his job, he is no more privileged, or regarded, than any other citizen. In short, we do not stand in awe with feelings of inferiority to a person in a position of organizational superiority; he is just another individual trying to earn his living. When he is not acting in his official capacity, he has no power to influence us. We have no need to fear him or be paralyzed in thought or action in his presence.

In summary, then, we invent and use psychological authority figures so that we can abdicate personal responsibility by putting it on their backs. Our object, in such projections of the mind, is to avoid having to keep and use our own initiative when confronted with situations. It is a way of reverting to childhood responses, by which we seek protection of parents when exposed to threat. In other words, psychological authority figures are our own invention and exist only in the head of the individual who evokes them. Their sole use to us is so that we can pass the buck at times when we ought to be acting on a self-reliant basis.

### » THE DESIRE TO BE LOVED VS LOVING

The person who seeks to be loved is himself not a lover; he is grasping, ungiving, possessive and worst of all—hungry. One who is a lover, on the other hand, is content; he feels no lack and has no need to seek anything in return. The two are psychologically worlds apart. The one is suffering from the acquisitive, getting attitude of mind, whereas the other is a giver. The craving to be loved grows out of a feeling of inadequacy, poverty and emptiness. But the condition of loving arises out of a feeling of fullness, adequacy, and affirmation.

Love has no object. It makes no demands. It is a condition of fullness that flows over everything. Like rain, it falls impartially on all alike. It demands nothing for itself and allows everything to fulfill itself in its own way. It is without a need to control others or to withhold itself. It lives and lets live.

The kind of love that has an object is merely possessiveness; it should not be called love at all. It wishes to acquire, hold, devour and exploit the object of its attention. When it is frustrated, it turns savagely with bitter hatred toward that which stands in its path to power and dominance. If it cannot possess, it wishes to destroy. Such love is a stick with two ends; one is called love and the other hate. It remains nothing more than two aspects of possessiveness, inseparable from the old theme of dominance-submission, enslavement and tyranny. In short, such love is only an extension into adult life of original, infantile dependence on someone to nourish and support us without cost or effort to ourselves.

### » FREEDOM FROM FEAR

Fear is not a thing in itself, nor can it be got rid of as if it were a separate thing. Fear is only the dark and terrifying shadow cast by the ambition for personal recognition. Ambition is desire, and desire brings the fear of not getting what we seek.

Just as it is not possible for a man to jump over his own shadow, it is likewise impossible for him to get rid of fear as a separate thing. To free himself from fear, he must first free himself from his goals aimed at winning rewards and recognition. Men's efforts to free themselves from fear fail because they try to erase the shadow and do not bother to remove the substance that casts the shadow. Only the man who has freed himself from the itch for rewards can ever be free of fear.

» PRIDE

The word pride is misleading. It produces endless confusion in some minds, as they often imagine they are called upon to maintain their pride in the face of others. Since they do not have a clear understanding of the real meaning of the term, they often find themselves trapped in destructive, negative, intransigent, resistant or nonproductive kinds of behavior in the belief that they are upholding their pride and that such support is vital to their welfare. A clear view of the situation we describe as pride is the best defense we can have against falling into the trap it represents.

Pride is a hostile, competitive game we play to maintain an illusion of personal superiority over others; it grows out of a begging attitude. Pride always indicates leaning on others' opinions and a lack of emotional self-reliance. It means we become confused and uncertain in seeking personal recognition, praise, support, indulgence or emotional subsidy from those around us. The term "ego" and the term "pride" both point to the same defect in our character; both are beggars, outgrowths of a lack of self-reliance. The person whose initiative and confidence grows out of his own ability to function independently without looking to others for direction or support has no need for pride or ego-recognition begging. His autonomous, independent activity is its own reward. He has *his own* approval, so that he does not need to beg it from another.

Pride is just another of the many forms of envious, competitive behavior. The main emotion that accompanies pride is self-pity. Pride is competitive because we cannot endure someone else being given higher recognition than we are. We always want to be above others in preferment or our pride is hurt. "There shall be no other gods before me," is our motto. Since it is based on envy and competition—and grows out of the fear that someone will be preferred to us—it dominates, degrades and dulls our minds, so that we lose our freedom and are not able to spend our attention on productive, independent activities basic to our survival. The greater our pride, the less our creative, productive potentiality becomes, and in the same ratio. We become inwardly sterile as we invest our outward efforts to support our pride, until we are naked under a mink coat.

Pride, then, condemns the individual to emotional

sterility. He lives and dies with the feeling that he is unfulfilled. He has only a continuing feeling of being impoverished. The recognition he begs or wrings from others does not reward, fill or warm him. It only restimulates insecurity feelings, self-pity and a stronger demand for recognition and support. Pride is nothing more, then, than the begging attitude. It beggars us and is a friend of no one.

### » THE PERFECTIONIST

The perfectionist is the opposite of what he seems to be; his love of perfection is spurious. It is a game he plays against people to hide his desire to dominate and control those around him. It is a game of one-upmanship designed to put others down to a lower level, so that he can shine in comparison to them. It hides his sadistic, unsocial, tyrannical habit of mind and behavior. He insists that others play by his rules and then makes sure that they cannot achieve superiority over him in his field by raising the standard on them. He is a deeply fearful person who dares not improvise, invent, discover, play-by-ear or otherwise live spontaneously. He wants to protect himself by a barrier of rules, rituals and standards, so that he can never be judged as being less-than-perfect. He cannot exist in an atmosphere of live-and-let-live. Coexistence as an equal member of a group is impossible. He must find fault and blemish in everyone, so that he can eliminate them as being inferior and thus avoid cooperating with them.

The perfectionist, then, is in essence a chronic faultfinder who wants to place social distance between himself and others because of his fear of sharing and participating as an equal member of human society. The game he plays is known as Big Me and Little You. He disrupts and distracts the activity of others lest they surpass him in the esteem of those around him. His perfectionism seldom contributes anything original of value to a situation, since productivity is not his goal. He is only truly interested in being competitive and measuring himself enviously against all other men.

## » THE ILLUSION OF OUTSIDE AUTHORITY

All that appears to be outside authority is an illusion of the mind which was formed in childhood and has not been destroyed by the light of common sense. There is no such thing as outside authority. We are born alone, we live alone and we die alone. We all are peers, but no one is a superior. Each is autonomous in his own life. The *illusion* of outside authority appears as a mirage before our senses only when we wish to escape personal responsibility and are *seeking someone to blame*. We invent such illusory figures when we want to *abdicate our own initiative* and be able to point to these synthetic gods as the source of our misfortune if we do not succeed in our own larcenous ambitions for aggrandizement and exploitation.

Man creates outside authority figures for the same reason that he creates idols. The primitive man and the childish man are alike; they are deeply fearful of uncertainty in life and their ability to achieve their aims. The primitive digs up mud to fashion it into an image and calls it "God." He puts it on a pedestal so that its head is *higher than his own*. Then he abdicates and prays to this image of his own creation—to this god to do favors for him—to send rain, crops and fruit. But these prayers are not really supplications at all. They are commands and demands hidden in a begging voice. The child is whining for his supper, and he calls his whining reverence "prayer," or "worship," whereas it is only abdication of his own personal responsibility. He sets up his outside authority figures so that he can make infantile demands *for them to take care of him*—as his parents did when he was little. And he becomes rebellious, angry or resentful if the god he has made does not answer his demands. His apparent submission to, and fear of, such imaginary outside authority figures stops immediately as soon as he faces the realization that they exist only inside his head, as his own invention, and do not exist in the outside world or have the power to grant him gifts. No power exists outside an individual that can damage him. All that helps or hurts him is of his own invention. Each of us must be a lamp unto his own feet—else he remains in darkness. Each must finally be his own and only final authority. He can never delegate nor abdicate this fundamental position. His strength is internal, never external.

### » HAPPINESS IS NOT A FEELING: IT IS A CONDITION

Contrary to common belief, *happiness is not a feeling.* Those who imagine it is a feeling frequently spend a lifetime searching to achieve happiness, as though it can be captured by pursuit, strategy or effort. All they achieve from this grasping attitude is ultimate disappointment, because happiness is *made up of nothing at all.* It is a condition of being. It either is or it is not. It cannot be made, achieved or found, as if it were some external thing to be gained by search. It forever eludes those who try to grasp it.

Happiness cannot be known to us consciously, strange as that may seem. The moment we ask ourselves if we are happy, happiness is gone. We become immediately fearful and critical of our situation. Conscious examination leads us to feel that everything is less than perfect, or inadequate. Suddenly we see the hole in the doughnut. This gives rise to the old saying, "Happiness does not take its own pulse."

Happiness is wholly unconscious and far beyond the grasp of the mind. It is a total condition, not conscious. For the present, we have transcended our need for personal recognition and are seeking nothing from the world around us. We are in a state of being, not in the anxiety of becoming. Happiness is the condition that ensues when all seeking, grasping or desire for anything *outside the immediate situation* has stopped. It is the condition that exists when all feeling of poverty, need, insufficiency and comparison has stopped—a condition when desire is absent. It is the miror surface of a pond when no wind blows. This explains why it disappears the moment we try to grasp it by any effort of wish or will.

The common difficulty of man is that he has tasted pain and pleasure. Man has mistakenly believed that he can seek the stimulation of pleasure and somehow avoid pain. If we do not realize that the *pursuit of pleasure ends in pain,* we shall seek ways to multiply our pleasures and end up increasing our anxiety and feeling of emptiness.

Unhappiness is the painful tension that is inseparable from ambition and desire. To rid ourselves of pain, we spend endless energy pursuing pleasure and buy endless things in the hope that they will result in happiness. But we find that this process is as impossible as it is for a man to get rid of his own shadow. The more we pursue pleasure, the more happiness eludes us, and we defeat ourselves by having discouragement added to our pain.

Happiness seeks nothing outside itself; pleasure seeks constant rewards and tidbits. Happiness simply *is.* It has no cause and does not depend on outside props to hold it up. It is a condition when there is no separation between the doer and the doing, when there is a release from self-criticism, self-evaluation, self-consciousness. When the ego is nonexistent to make comparisons or seek approval. The moment an individual reaches out of this unconscious condition and brings conscious thinking, evaluation, planning, desire or ambition back into the situation, the spell is broken. He is plunged back into the hell of endless seeking, the desire for rewards, personal assurances, compensations and securities.

Pleasure is a counterfeit invention of the conscious mind, a spurious substitute for happiness. Just as counterfeit money tends to drive out sound currency, so does the pursuit of pleasure tend to lead us farther away from the condition of letting go that is basic to happiness. Happiness can exist only when effort, pursuit and grasping fade away.

Happiness lies beyond the effort of the human will. It does not respond to wishful thinking. It becomes the living now only when we finally let go our grasp on things and walk on, seeking nothing to add to our stature or carry with us in any way.

### » WILL POWER VS CREATIVITY

Will power is the use of effort, determination or violence to achieve a goal. It is a part of the desire for ego recognition. It has the aim to expand the ego, to achieve a point of vantage from which to dominate, exploit, control, intimidate the world around us. Things done by will power are blind and usually arise from negative conformity. They can never be spontaneous or original—things arising from spontaneity and the spirit. Will power springs from wishful thinking, or the feeling of insufficiency, which grows into a lust for dominance. Spontaneity and spirit are the flowering of a free mind that know no feelings of inferiority or inadequacy.

Creativity is the healthy, effortless breathing of a free

mind. Creativity is like the wind that comes from where we do not know and blows wherever it wishes. Creativity is the spirit of the picnic, which has no pattern to obey. Creativity is play activity; it has no need to prove anything to anyone or to win any rewards. It knows no discipline and reveres no one. Creativity is its own reward. It takes no thought of how it will move and follows no pattern except its own.

Will power, however, is tense, grasping and anxious for rewards. It knits its brows and doubts its strength. Such anxiety dulls the mind. Spontaneity *happens* when we are not thinking and thus is free of anxiety. Suddenly, there it *is*. It acts out of its own center. When will power, which is only another name for wishful thinking, enters the scene, then spirit, playfulness and creativity depart at once.

## » THE HATER IS ONLY A DISAPPOINTED LOVER

Love and hate are but two different ways of depending on someone else. Love (eros) is gratified dependency. Hate is our resentment at being frustrated at being dependent. There is a love (agape) which has no opposite and seeks no favors or return. It exists when we are wholly impartial in our interest and are willing to live-and-let-live in coexistence. Such love makes no demands and seeks no benefits, since it arises from our acceptance of the situation or person without any desire to change it in any way. We are in a state of affirmation or acceptance of reality, and living, at least for that moment, in the here-and-now.

## » DOES SUCCESS EXIST?

Success does not exist in reality; it is only a purely competitive concept, idea or ideal on which many base their way of life. It denies joy in the present and promises life and fulfillment at some future time. There is no joy in the process of moment-to-moment living, since it is regarded only as a means to an end, the goal of success!

Thousands of years ago the *Bhagavad Gita* recognized the evil of working for rewards. It says: "You have the right to work but for work's sake only. You have no right to the fruits of work. Desire for the fruits of work should never be your motive in working. . . . Renounce attachment to the fruits. . . . Work done with anxiety about results is far inferior to work done without such anxiety in the calm of self-surrender. They who work selfishly for results are miserable." In short, pleasure departs when we seek something in some distant future time.

### » INSPIRATION—IS IT NECESSARY?

Many seek inspiration from books, leaders, art, music and other outside sources. But people who habitually seek inspiration are given to the habit of wishful thinking. They live in danger. Inspiration is a form of outside influence and intoxication on which they become dependent as a drug. They use it to hide their fear and lack of self-sufficiency from themselves, and under its influence they feel brave and confident. But when real situations face them and they are not prepared, inspiration lets them down in the early dawn when fears crowd around them.

### » CLIMBERS AND DOERS

The world is divided into two kinds of people—climbers and doers. The climbers' aim in life is to get to the top of anything they can climb onto. They are the hungry ones. They are born hungry; they live hungry; they die hungry. But they still climb to the pointless end. They do not know nor ask why they climb. Doers create and shape their own world inside themselves. They explore, produce and build out of the fulness of their independence. They feel no need to seek or beg from anyone. They live in a state of discovery of the unfolding unknown—like the Lewis and Clark expedition.

### » HAVE YOU, OR ARE YOU, A PROBLEM?

A person may have a problem or be one. The person who is a problem does not feel that he has a problem. He gets along splendidly exploiting and taking from others who put up with him. The person who puts up with him is the person who has the problem—the problem of providing support for the one who is a problem. In short, it takes both of them to make it possible for the one to fail!

Those who are problems have no incentive to improve their own behavior, so long as it continues to pay them by taking support out of others. They run away from discipline or treatment.

The one who needs the treatment is the one on whom they lean to exploit. The misguided victim must be taught to be more independent himself and to refuse to be exploited by providing mistaken subsidies.

When the exploiting individual is refused profit from his victim, he can no longer continue to be a problem. He suddenly finds that *he* has a problem—how to manage on his own without assistance!

» OWNERS OR SHAREHOLDERS

Each individual is like a company that has one hundred shares of stock. As long as you can maintain 51 percent or more, you cannot be voted out of control of the business. Even though you may have to pay dividends to outside stockholders for shares they hold in you, the final vote on policy remains with you as long as you keep your stock.

In reality, each of us has one hundred shares and each of us is stuck with them. We may believe mistakenly, or even pretend, that others have control of a voting majority of our stock, but this is only our own illusion or delusion, based on wishful thinking. It is a device of ours to flee from full responsibility for the one hundred shares by trying to transfer at least part of them to others. Since it is not possible to rid ourselves of a single share of our original investment, we are charged with full responsibility at all times. It is for this vital reason that we may never delude ourselves that we can pass our initiative, or our authority, to someone else to exercise in our behalf and for our own welfare. They have no responsibility for us.

## » SELF-JUSTIFICATION DOES NOT CONVINCE

What can one do if someone belittles him or otherwise expresses a biased, poor opinion about him? It is of no use to fight back and deny or refute the attack. Even if the person recants his statements when confronted, any effort to convince him against his will allows him to be of the same opinion still, as the saying goes. What shall, or can, one do about it?

As with all else, we must be independent of his opinion. It must give him some deep competitive satisfaction to think, or feel, hostile to us. Perhaps he is envious of us and wants to elevate himself by putting us down with others. Whatever his reason for the attack on us, we know that he is hostile and will probably remain so in spite of anything we can do about it. It is a free country, however, so we must grant him his right to feel as he does about us. And we might as well be generous and grant him the right to say what he wishes, since we can't stop him.

Our main problem will be our dependence on his good

opinion. This is more than our concern about any harm his words may bring us. To free ourself of the hypnotic hold his attack may have on us, we must invite him to be our guest and to feel or do exactly as he pleases to amuse himself. By assuming the role of the host to him, in our own mind, we free ourselves of any temptation to brainwash him into thinking or saying that which we feel he ought to feel about us. Being a host to him frees us from having a negatively dependent "love affair" with him and from being tied to someone who was not of our own choosing, At least, it frees us to pick our own friends and not be tied to those we fear.

### » EMOTIONS ARE NOT REASONS

Most people are ruled by their emotions and think nothing strange about the fact that they have so little to say about their own lives. How could anyone ruled by his emotions be anything other than a *victim* of his own emotions. Emotions are not reasons; they are only the steam we generate to drive us toward our objectives, which we would pursue even if we put no steam behind them. Emotions only make us go faster.

The nature and direction of our actions are determined

not by our emotions but by our basic degree of self-reliance. We can't have more than we can carry on our back! Our responses are not determined by what problem is confronting us. We respond depending on whether we plan to face it *by ourselves independently* or whether we plan to look around and find some other back on which to put it. Self-reliance must be our *starting point* from which we work. There is no anxiety in a self-reliant approach to problems; there is only the spirit of adventure and discovery; a "Let's see what happens" approach to life.

It is obvious, then, that the emotions we call up in this adventuresome frame of mind become a wind at our backs to blow us on our way. We will create no disjunctive, or distracting, emotions or resistance, and we will welcome with pleasure whatever happens on the way. When we resist, it is like trying to sail with no wind. We create a slowdown in all our acts and feelings.

Most people use their likes and dislikes as a compass to find which way the emotional wind is blowing. They are bound to pile up on the rocks of reality. Likes and dislikes are merely conditioned responses we *learned in childhood* and have no significance, except that they are now habits! It is not at all remarkable that an Eskimo likes blubber, or a cannibal human flesh! But it doesn't mean that they cannot be just as happy eating other things if they are not hopelessly dependent on their old habits of likes and dislikes to guide them. Strong dependence on our likes and dislikes is *a sure sign of immaturity.*

There is a remarkable Zen poem that deals with this problem of dependence. In essence it says:

*The perfect way is without difficulty,*
*—it avoids picking and choosing.*
*Only when you stop liking and disliking*
*will all be clearly understood.*
*A split hair's difference,*
*and you set heaven and earth apart!*
*If you want to get the plain truth,*
*Be not concerned with right and wrong.*
*The conflict between right and wrong*
*Is the sickness of the mind.*

Most of us guard and protect our likes and dislikes as if they were more precious than life itself; we will even die to protect our right to indulge our appetites. We protect them as absolutes that we must use to measure and guide our whole stay on earth! If a like is threatened, we whip up a whole storm of emotion to scare off the invader who threatens it. We fly up in arms, whereas nothing is threatened except some prejudicial habit we formed at mother's knee.

When likes or dislikes are threatened, we have a choice of treating them as we would a live spark that blew in the window and fell on the rug—we can step on it and immediately put it out, or we can get down and blow on it until it fans into a flame and burns us up with the whole house. We control them; they do not control us. No one is ever carried away by his emotions. It takes a lot of effort and application on our part to blow the average like-dislike into a sustained kind of uproar, or warfare, to be carried on against all odds. Emotions die on the vine if we do not water them with our tears!

### » COMMUNICATION

We speak about communication but seldom understand what a limited thing it is, even at best. Those who know and understand a thing respond to those who also know it as they do. But it is almost impossible to communicate with someone *who does not know*. If you try to explain what the color white is to a blind man and tell him it is like snow, he will understand that white is wet and cold. It can never be possible for him to know what white *looks like* by giving him visual analogies, because he cannot *directly experience* the color people with vision call white.

Understanding is a wholly personal phenomenon. Even for the individual who is able to see white directly, the significance and meaning of white is something ever changing and personal to him. Though he can talk about it to another person, and the other person may seem to understand what is being said, it may become evident later that we never really communicated at any level deeper than a shallow one.

We are born alone, we live alone and we die alone. Many hope to escape this common fate of all individuals by seeking to understand, or more impossible still, to be understood by, those around them. The desire to be understood sets up tensions of frustration when we discover that the fancied closeness we believe we have created with someone leaves us miles apart at the action level of experience. We see in a flash that we have only been talking to ourselves at times, when we thought we were expressing, or explaining, things clearly and were being fully understood by the listener. We react with fear and surprise as if we found ourselves on the edge of a cliff.

Wisdom lies in realizing that each person lives in a private world which can never be wholly bridged or transcended. As with the planets of our solar system, we can see them and make inferences of their common origin and relationship, but we cannot know the real meaning, or condition, of any one of them. Nor could we live as we are constituted on them if we got there.

The individual is as unique as the planet on which he lives and would be an artifact and unfit for survival on another planet. The understanding of each individual is unique in this same way. Only *he* is able to function within the elements of *his own understanding* and, thus, from there, make changes in *his own behavior*. Togetherness is an illusion we sometimes conjure up to escape the need to develop self-reliance. Togetherness is the blind leading the blind.

### » WHAT IS FRIENDSHIP?

A group of alcoholic patients in an alcoholic clinic were discussing personal relationships. One mentioned the difficulty of finding a real friend anywhere in this world. Most of them snorted and jeered over anyone naive enough to imagine a real friend existed in this world. A few of them insisted that a person might have at least one true friend. A lone individual thought it might even be possible to have two true friends. No one could imagine having more than that.

It was a hot discussion; they deplored the lack of integrity to be encountered in the world, as they saw it. The discussion leader finally had them try to define the qualities of a true friend. In the end, they concluded that a true friend was one who would give them the shirt off his back.

Alfred Adler pointed out that there is so much that is

unconscious in our consciousness and so much that is conscious in our unconsciousness that it is useless to try to separate them as such. But we must see the direction in which both are pointing. These alcoholic patients were unconsciously telling us that they sought friends only among those whom they could exploit right down to taking the shirt off their backs! Their whole estimate of friendship was based on, or debased to, what they could get out of it for themselves. In short, a friend was someone who would not resist their exploitation; they would reject those who would resist, as their refusal would be evidence that, *if we cannot use them, they are not our friends*!

The truth is that most relationships we call friendships are seldom more than mutual-advantage, or mutual-exploitation, pacts, which dissolve as soon as the element of mutual advantage disappears on either side. When it is no longer emotionally or physically profitable to know each other, we drift apart. Mutual assistance—cooperation—is the basis of social and personal survival, so that any relationship lacking in mutual advantage cannot survive without damage to those who participate. Our real friends, then, are not those from whom we can get this or that at discount prices or for nothing. Our real friends are those for whom we have a warm willingness to participate on a live-and-let-live basis. The number of our friendships is limited only by our ability to be a friend; not to those who give us the shirt off their back.

### » BE THE HOST, NOT THE GUEST, IN LIFE

Many people feel uncomfortable in social situations. Meeting strangers is difficult for them. They feel inept in the relationship and do not know what to do. This is because they habitually think, feel and behave in a passive-receptive way toward the outside world and turn their initiative over to anyone who will pick it up to carry for them. They live in this world as if they believed it was right for them to be always the guest, never the host. They see nothing unusual or unfair in their habit of abdicating initiative and expecting the other person to exercise it for their benefit.

The role of the child is the role of a guest in the home; everything is done to and for him—at least in the beginning. But maturity demands the opposite role of us. We must expect to spend ourselves and to give out to those around us, not to continue the passive-receptive role of the child, who sits waiting for others to enrich and entertain him.

In social contacts, then, we must consciously behave as if those present are our honored guests whom we have invited and we must take care of them. We must go halfway toward them and not let them hang in mid-air. We shall not be in mid-air either as we shall be too busy dealing with the realities of the emerging now to think about being self-conscious. We learn to manipulate the impersonal demands of the situation and, in this way, do not block ourselves.

### » YOU CAN'T AFFORD AN EGO

The ego is the only part of us that hurts or gets hurt in relationships. Contrary to common belief, that we must laboriously build up ego strength to meet the world, the ego is a beggar habitually craving for prestige, support, pampering, recognition and special privilege. The ego is something to get rid of.

Like any beggar, the ego is hurt when someone passes by and does not drop something in the begging bowl. It feels rejected, ignored and put down; it feels that it has been seriously damaged in a vital part and deprived of something essential. No one is so high in emotional assets that he can afford to support either an ego of his own or the ego of another person. One's mental health is in inverse ratio to the size of his ego and the demands for pampering it makes upon one.

The hypersensitive person is at a total disadvantage in this world. Trying to support the greedy demands necessary to an inflated ego is like trying to support a heroin addiction. Every day it takes more flattery and support, and costs more effort, even if one has to turn to crime to do it. The ego is insatiable: there is no limit to its appetite for praise. It is a tyrant to the one who has it.

## » GUILT FEELINGS: A PLEA FOR IRRESPONSIBILITY

Guilt feelings are only a plea to maintain a position of total irresponsibility and to hold on to the plea to abdicate our own initiative. To feel guilty is to be afraid of being found out and of subsequently losing face, or of probable punishment, like a child with jam on its face. It is not our high moral nature that produces guilt feelings in us but our fear of the opinion of others. It is our lack of self-confidence and self-reliance. The person who is living fully on his own initiative and responsibility will not have to do anything for which he will later feel ashamed or guilty.

## » TEARS FOR THE BELOVED EGO

Sorrow is only a form of anger. Anger arises when we have been leaning on, or planning to lean on, something —and it is suddenly denied us. Our first reaction, when our crutch breaks and we fall forward on our face, is to go into a rage. If there is someone we can blame, that is our next step. If we can punish him, that is even better. But if there is no one we can hit out at, then we must swallow our rage; it has no other choice but to churn around inside us. This internal form of rage, or anger, we express as sorrow, sadness or depression. These are three words for the same displeasure.

All the tears we shed in sorrow are tears shed only for ourselves. The self-sufficient person sheds no tears and has no regrets about the past. He has no need to mourn his losses since he has not been leaning on them. He does not go into a depression. Tears are shed over loss, not for the dear departed.

## » SWAMP OR TRACTOR: WHICH WILL WIN?

People divide themselves into two categories. We are predominantly either Swamps or Tractors, depending on our habitual pattern of activity. Tractors are those who are highly active and usually like to charge into problems or situations with much energy. They enjoy showing strength and dominance over both people and situations. Swamps, on the other hand, usually have a low degree of activity. When they are faced with problems or demands on them, they usually present a total passivity, which engulfs everything in the hope that the problem will bog down and sink out of sight—if they just sit and ignore it long enough. This passivity is so irritating to Tractors that they frequently charge in and solve the problem for Swamps. The Swamp is thus one-up on the Tractor, and knows it! For some unknown reason, the Swamp is called a "weak character"—in spite of the fact that he wins without effort or investment on his part.

Tractors often feel challenged by the passivity of Swamps and decide to teach such passive individuals to become Tractors, like themselves. Such encounters always end in the defeat of the Tractor, since the Swamp is always able to win out. When a real tractor runs into a swamp, regardless of how powerful it is, it eventually runs out of gas and sinks down out of sight. In human relationships passivity can always win out over activity in a contest of wills. Those misguided individuals who have decided that they can reform a person with a weak character find themselves in an impossible situation.

The Tractor (sadist) believes he is stronger than the Swamp (masochist) and exerts all his power to suppress, punish and degrade the weak one. But the Swamp enjoys proving that he can take everything the Tractor dishes out—and then some! He comes up fresh as a daisy, to prove the relative impotence of the Tractor, who has run out of gas in the self-defeating process of trying to influence the Swamp!

This does not prove that it is bad to have a high degree of activity! On the contrary. Every problem demands activity, and the person without activity is seriously crippled in this world. We should develop and maintain a high degree of activity. But we must avoid the mistake of the Tractor. We must maintain our initiative and not go about trying to influence others to submit to our will.

# *Reflections*

Every goal we set restricts us. It limits, selects and determines the means it uses to accomplish its own ends. Any goal sets its own built-in price. What it excludes may be worth more than what it achieves. Goals are either *on* or *off*. They by-pass all that does not serve their aims. They invent whatever is necessary to do the job. The running deer created the arrow that shot through its heart; the arrow created the bow to send it to its mark; and the deer, the arrow and the bow created the skill of the man who used them.

»

Revenge, retaliation and similar forms of hitting back clearly indicate dependence. It shows that we lost our initiative to someone who used our dependence against us. And it shows that we have not regained our initiative if we are still attached enough to want to pay that someone back for using us. If each one hangs on to his own key to the executive's toilet, he will not have to raise his hand and ask permission to leave the room for necessary functions pertaining to himself. Instead of planning retaliation, one ought to ask: "What could I have done in the first place, had I remained self-reliant and not leaned on someone else to run my errand for me?" Revenge renews the tie to the hated individual; it increases the original attachment instead of resolving it.

»

Life can no more be caught in a set of rules, regulations, disciplines or formulae than one can catch the wind in a bag. Any attempt to trap life into a formula or catch wind in a bag is futile. The first turns out dead forms and the latter turns wind into a bag of old, stale air.

»

We cannot take action until our mind gives the body a clear direction and command. Moves must be toward or away from, up or down, yes or no. The body cannot stand up and sit down simultaneously. Each movement is either on a clear command out of our own initiative, or we move at the initiative of another person. We must be constantly aware whether we initiate our action or take our direction from outside.

»

We like to believe that we are split into the Good I and the Bad Me! That the Good I toils far into the night to improve the incorrigible behavior of the unregenerate Bad Me! This imagined split is a convenient illusion we maintain to avoid having to take full responsibility for our mistaken habits. It is a good alibi but, when we are finally ready to let go of a bad habit, we drop the nonsense about a split in our personality; we accept the habit as our responsibility all the way. The only way to stop a bad habit is to stop it! When we honestly have a bellyful of a bad habit, it is not difficult to let go of its apparent hold on us.

»

There is no up without down, good apart from bad, end without a beginning. In reality, every end is a beginning. Opposites cannot be separated. They never lose sight of each other, and we deceive ourselves if we believe we can have the one without paying for the other.

»

One is about as happy as he makes up his mind to be, according to a quotation of Lincoln's. In truth, happiness has no causes. It is a decision—which can be made consciously or unconsciously on the part of the individual—that life is worth living, even though it is less than perfect! A person who feels this way about life does not go into shock when he encounters difficulty, but assumes that it will pass, as does everything else. He is neither optimistic nor pessimistic, since they are two crutches used by those lacking self-reliance. He walks on and lives the hot or the cold as it comes—and decides that anything is better than being apathetic or in habitual resistance.

»

Asking why we do things is of small use, because there are no causes for our behavior. The answers we invent for ourselves are seldom useful. We try to rationalize the question because it has been asked. If you ask a silly question you get a silly answer! Why do ducks have flat feet? To stamp out forest fires! Then why do elephants have flat feet? To stamp out burning ducks!

»

Nervousness, irritability, hypersensitivity and reactivity are separate words that all mean the same thing: we are being frustrated in our efforts to manipulate someone. They won't stand still for us nor respond to our controls. We do not like their obvious insubordination to our wishes.

»

Hope is a whore, a cheat, a deceiver. She seduces victims and makes unwarranted, ungrounded promises so that they lean on her—not on themselves. Hope is merely wishful thinking, or a longing, for Santa Claus to bail us out. Hope entices us to postpone living in the present as if there were a future on which we could depend. The more one depends on hope, the more one fears for his situation. Hope deferred dries up like a raisin in the sun. When Pandora opened the box of evils, war, pestilence, disease, famine and all their kin emerged to flood the world. The greatest evil came out last. It was hope—the great postponer, the tempter to abdication, the death blow to initiative. Hope is fear of the present.

»

Keep track of your initiative. Know where it is at all times, the same as if it were in your pocketbook. It is far more important than your money. Is it with you now? Or did you toss it to the fellow next to you and expect that he will guard it for you? Did you expect he would cherish it and pass it back to you when it suits your purpose?

»

Let others be right half the time, even when you know that they are mistaken. After all, they did not hire you to be their tutor. Resist your temptation to show them up and expose their error. They do not want to be put into an inferior light by you.

»

To be either for or against something is to be tied to it; one is not free in either case. One aspect is not more free than the other essentially. The same is true of love or hate, like or dislike, seek or avoid. If we either love or hate someone, or something, we are dependent on it. In short, we abdicate, and our initiative lies outside the self in someone else—where it doesn't belong.

»

If you seek to gain anything from another person, you cannot be friends. Friendship is free of seeking for personal advantage for oneself. It is neither mutually exploitative nor mutually possessive. There are no mutual controls or manipulations; each is free to be himself. There is no competition between real friends and thus no ground for hurt feelings. Only so can there be a free friendship in which one does not set limits or controls on the other.

»

The manipulator is always outside the world he is manipulating; he is not able to be a participator in it. Nor does he have any world of his own. He can only watch in envy as he pulls the strings and watches others dance while they get the fun and exercise. Manipulators are fearful of getting wet by life. They fear direct involvement.

»

Arguments are attempts to manipulate and subordinate others. We argue only if we feel weak. If we feel we are in the dominating position, we do not bother to argue. Arguing is a form of nagging and is always a clear sign of dependency. When we give up trying to influence others, we have no further need to argue with them.

»

Those who seek power do so because they feel weak. The more they seek power the more they frighten themselves. The more power they get, the more they feel they have to lose. Their situation grows worse with power than it was in the beginning.

»

The person in search of greatness lives only for appearances, for things, for the opinions of others and for recognition, so that he misses the substance of life itself. He laboriously cracks the nut, eats the shell and throws the nut away. He believes that others do the same!

»

Ideals are only wishful thinking. Such thinking rots the fabric of the mind. It destroys the ability to see and act clearly and spontaneously. Intuitive action becomes impossible. Visceral, gut-action response is thwarted. Only a pale, intellectual imitation of vitality takes its place.

»

When is a man a free agent? When has he a free mind? You are free the moment you do not look outside yourself for someone to solve your problems. You will know that you are free and feel free inside yourself when you no longer blame anyone, or anything, not even yourself, for unhappiness. You will know you are free because you accept life as a postman accepts the weather; he just walks his rounds and does not make a problem out of it.

»

Masters and slaves, followers and leaders, conspire for mutual enslavement and abdication of personal responsibility; neither knows how to stand alone without the other to hold him up. There are two worlds—the world of the dedicated and the world of the abdicated. The dedicated spend themselves, their time, their energy and their spirit; they are doers. The abdicated withhold themselves in a hope that they can save themselves and somehow add to their life by not spending it. Time, money, life, spirit—none of these has any value unless we *spend* them.

»

Anything done out of a sense of duty is done from outside initiative and is an act of subordination. It is not fair to do your duty *for* others, since you will hate them for making you do it—and then punish them out of retaliation and resentment because you feel dominated by them. They will be better off in the end without your act of submission, since they will escape your hidden revenge.

»

Compensations do not compensate. At least not at the psychological level. A weak body can be strengthened by exercise. That is successful compensation at the physical level. But if a person developed the habit of feeling inferior about his weakness, then the feelings remain even after physical compensation has taken place and he continues to feel like a second-class citizen. His memory of past humiliations remains alive in his mind, like a ghost at a banquet.

»

Ambition for recognition and rewards breeds lies and deception—the desire to make a good impression. We try to fool others! Or fool ourselves that we are fooling them! Mostly the latter is the result.

»

Addictions are nothing more than exaggerated habits which we inflate to hide the shallowness of our inner life, our lack of independence and self-sufficiency. We use them to ward off loneliness. Addictions are props for lagging self-esteem and always are distress signals of a dying initiative.

»

New England has always had a strong tradition of self-reliance and has prized the ability to survive under hardship. In the mountains of Vermont, the natives have a saying: "My feet don't stand around while my body is being abused."

»

Initiative is a spontaneous response to a confronting situation, where we deal with the demands without evasion. If there is dirt on the floor, we clean it up instead of stepping over it or trying to get someone else to clean it for us.

»

Self-reliance *is* initiative. You must start with initiative, keep initiative and end with initiative. Your welfare is your own at all times. If you do give up your initiative, you have no one to blame except yourself—and your complaints are not justified, since you invited and earned the consequences.

»

A conformist is a person who has no initiative of his own. He is like an expensive car with enormous horsepower under the hood—but he has no self-starter and cannot get going without a push or pull from someone else.

# *Bibliography*


Adler, Alfred. *Understanding Human Nature.* World Publishing Company, 1927.

——*What Life Should Mean to You.* Little, Brown & Company, 1931.

Beecher, Marguerite and Willard. *Parents on the Run.* Julian Press, 1955. DeVorss (paperback), 1983.

Benedict, Ruth. *Patterns of Culture.* Houghton Mifflin Company, 1934.

Berne, Eric, M.D. *Games People Play.* Grove Press, 1964.

Chase, Stuart. *The Tyranny of Words.* Harcourt, Brace & Company, 1938.

Emerson, Ralph Waldo. *Essays.* Random House, 1938.

Krishnamurti, J. *Commentaries.* Vols. I, II & III. Harper & Row, 1956, 1958, 1960.

Lao Tzu. *Tao Teh King.* Interpreted by Archie Bahm. Frederick Ungar, 1958.

Meade, Margaret. *New Lamps for Old.* William Morrow & Company, 1956.

Vaihinger, Hans. *The Philosophy of 'As If.'* Harcourt, Brace & Company, 1924.

Watts, Alan. *The Spirit of Zen.* London: John Murray, 1936.

——*The Wisdom of Insecurity.* Pantheon, 1949.

Whitman, Walt. *Leaves of Grass.* The Viking Press, 1945.